echoes and entrances

Finding Voice in Language Not Yet Our Own

Allison Zhang

For English language learners everywhere, and for those who walk beside them.

contents

about the author

Allison Zhang is a Chinese-American writer whose work explores the intersections of language, memory, and belonging. Growing up in Los Angeles as an immigrant and an identical twin, she was once an English language learner herself, an experience that shaped her deep love for storytelling and her belief that words shape identity. Her writing is inspired by the journeys of English language learners and the resilience found in everyday moments.

introduction

"You can't teach language in a void. It's about power, identity, and survival."

Ofelia García

When I moved from Shanghai to Los Angeles in elementary school, I didn't know the term "English language learner." I only knew the anxiety.

At school, I sat in classrooms where I couldn't follow the lesson. I didn't understand the jokes, didn't know when it was my turn to speak. I couldn't ask for help. Not because I didn't want to, but because I didn't yet have the words. There were no ESL classes in my school. Just a maze of expectations I had to navigate alone.

I was one of millions. Today, over 5 million English language learners (ELLs) are enrolled in U.S. public schools. Yet a disproportionate number are placed in under-resourced classrooms, mislabeled as slow, or silenced by the pressure to assimilate. I didn't understand that systemic failure. I just thought I was behind.

So I read.

I read obsessively—menus, picture books, novels, street signs, shampoo bottles. I read because it was the only way to stay afloat in a language that was not mine, in a country that seemed to have no room for the pauses I made between words.

"Language is not just words. It's a culture, a tradition, a unification of a community."

—Noam Chomsky

By high school, I was fluent. But fluency doesn't erase memory. I still remembered what it felt like to be the child who couldn't decode a class assignment, who feared roll call because her name would be mangled or ignored. I remembered what it felt like to be misunderstood not for what I said, but for how I said it.

That's why I started Literacy for ELL, a student-led nonprofit rooted in one simple belief: English learners deserve more than survival. They deserve access, opportunity, and dignity. Since its founding, we've reached over 500 ELLs across six countries, donated 6,000+ books, and built a community centered on the transformative power of literacy.

This book was born out of that same belief.

This book is for the students who know how much courage it takes to ask a question in a language not your own.

It's for the families who translate bills, report cards, and government forms late into the night.

It's for the educators trying their best with too few tools.

It's for the advocates and translators and whisperers between worlds.

Introduction

"The limits of my language mean the limits of my world."

—Ludwig Wittgenstein

This book does not present one story. It offers many: short stories, poems, fragments, field guides, research, and real interviews that I conducted—all to explore what it means to live in translation. You'll find moments of struggle, such as a missed joke, a botched interview, a child left out of a group project. But also moments of power: the first time someone dares to speak. The day a book cracks open a door. The teachers and librarians who listen harder.

It will also ask difficult questions. Why are ELL programs so underfunded? Why are language learners overrepresented in special ed referrals, and underrepresented in gifted programs? What myths about "accent," "fluency," and "belonging" still dictate the way we see—and missee—ELL students?

"Once you learn to read, you will be forever free."

—Frederick Douglass

I don't write this as an expert, but as a witness. As someone who once sat in the back of the classroom, and who now teaches, writes, and dreams in a language that once hurt to speak. This book is a tribute to all the learners still finding their voices—and a challenge to the systems that fail to hear them.

Introduction

To be an English language learner is not a deficit. It is not a delay.

It is a story of resistance, memory, translation, and growth.

This is mine.

And it belongs to all of us.

A. Zhang

part one

preface

Every journey into a new language begins with a first encounter—
a work spoken, a gesture misunderstood, a silence held too long.
These moments might seem small, but for those of us learning
English as another life, they leave marks as deep as footprints in
fresh concrete.

This section includes poems and reflections from those fragile
beginnings. It details the awkward choreography of belonging, the
courage it takes to speak, and the ways we carry home inside of us
even as we step into new worlds.

"First Encounters" is my map of those early crossings. Some
memories are soft; others sting. But each one proves that learning
a new language is more than vocabulary. It's a way of finding
ourselves again, piece by piece, in the echo of new words.

first encounters

"A new language is a new life."

Persian Proverb

Field Guide to Survival in English
compiled by a quiet student with a loud history

Entry #1: Hello
Say it like you mean it,
even if your mouth is still thinking in another language.
Smile, but not too wide.
Practice in the mirror until it no longer feels borrowed.

Entry #4: Answering Questions
Raise your hand.
Even if your answer is hiding behind the wrong verb
tense.
Even if your accent feels like a sore.
Mistakes mean you're alive here.

Entry #7: Lunch Tables
Do not sit until invited.
Even then, stay ready to move.
Learn the words for everything you love to eat
so no one gets to laugh before you finish your sentence.

Entry #9: Laughter
Sometimes it means kindness.
Sometimes it means warning.
Study the difference like vocabulary.
Pronounce your silence clearly.

Entry #12: Eye Contact
Do not hold it too long. It burns.
In your country, this was respect.
Here, it is suspicion.
Translate with your hands.

Entry #15: Group Projects
Speak once, even if your voice shakes.
Let the paper do the rest.
If they forget your name,
write it in capital letters across your part.

Entry #20: Saying Your Name
Say it whole.
Say it like the sky back home
untranslatable,
but still overhead.

Entry #25: Writing Essays
Choose words you can carry.
Not the longest, not the smartest
just the ones that do not betray you
when spoken aloud.

Entry #32: Teachers Who Try
You will recognize them.
They wait.
They listen.
They let you try.

Entry #36: Dreams in English
When they come,
do not panic.
It does not mean you are forgetting.
Only that the new language
is finally learning to love you back.

Allison Zhang

Accent
After Ocean Vuong

Don't worry.
Your accent is only an accent
until someone else repeats it.
Like how "shush" wears
the shirt of the first word
you were too afraid to say.
No one told you
"library" has an r
you're not supposed to swallow.
But you swallowed it anyway.
Because where you come from
the mouth is a river
& rivers are for keeping.
Child,
are you listening?
The most beautiful part
of your voice
is the part you thought was wrong.

Glossary for the Newly Displaced

flu•en•cy *(noun)*

1. the performance of comfort
2. what you fake to be believed
3. a wound so well hidden it sounds like confidence

ac•cent *(noun)*

1. a map traced in the mouth
2. proof of origin, even after forgetting
3. the reason they slow their words for you but not their judgment

e•ras•ure *(noun)*

1. the space between your name and how they say it
2. what remains when you answer to a nickname that isn't yours
3. standardized testing

sub•ject-verb a•gree•ment *(rule)*

1. I am
2. You are
3. We were never plural enough

tran•sla•tion *(noun)*

1. the betrayal that sounds like love
2. carrying your mother's voice into a room that never asked
3. an apology with grammar

mis•pro•nounce *(verb)*

1. to expose the body mid-sentence
2. to fail in front of a whiteboard
3. to be asked, again, where you're from

si•lence *(noun)*

1. the first language
2. survival
3. homework due tomorrow

par•ent *(noun)*

1. the one who learns through you
2. mouth full of longing they cannot name
3. calls the school but lets you talk

home *(noun)*

1. not here
2. not there
3. what you carry in tupperware, behind the new fridge

ESL *(abbreviation)*

1. English as a second life
2. English so they'll listen
3. English until you forget how to scream in your first

Pass (*verb*)

1. to answer without accent
2. to disappear with praise
3. to lose your country, perfectly

Allison Zhang

Dream in a Language I Forgot

I woke with a tongue
stitched to a cloud.
Soft, but pulling.
Every sound
was water I tried to drink
through a mirror.
The teacher handed me a paper
and the letters blinked
like a cousin I met in a dream
but couldn't touch.
I said window
and a flock of birds
flew out of my mouth—
none of them landed.
Someone asked my name
and the chalk
wrote it in snow.
When I looked down,
my hands were full
of unopened envelopes.
I gave one to my mother.
She smiled
like someone listening
from the bottom
of a lake.

learn

you better learn
like your name depends
on the way it sounds in someone else's mouth.
that pause between questions
is where courage begins.
consider that somebody once had to speak
with their hands
or their eyes
or a broken tongue
just so you could call a thing beautiful
and have someone believe you.
consider the first kid
in the first classroom
who didn't know how to say bathroom
but figured out a gesture
and made it through the day.
consider your mother
at the grocery store,
how she translated milk into money
with nothing but a look and a nod.
consider the teacher
who said your name almost right
and the feeling that gave you.
consider how fluency
is not the same as freedom
but close enough
to write a life with.
consider that every sentence you say
is a border you redraw,
that to answer in English
is to remember your first language
with your whole body.

Allison Zhang

consider how learning
is a way of running forward.
see how your words carry.
how you arrive.

Low Tide

The sky hangs in a single tone.
Clouds press against the water,
no edge between them.
The ocean moves without shine,
its surface broken only by breath:
long, regular,
measured.
A gull lands,
waits,
then walks the shoreline
as if something should be there.
Someone has left markings
in the wet sand.
Not letters, not words,
just attempts.
The waves arrive.
They do not praise.
They do not erase.
Only continue.
And in that rhythm,
a kind of permission.

inheritance and memory

"To have another language is to possess a second soul."

Charlemagne

Allison Zhang

You Always Said My Grammar Was Perfect
(Written in 2050)

Hi 妈
your voice on the voicemail still sounds like
California sun: flat, warm,
不靠近。
You ask how I'm doing.
Whether I'm still helping
kids with their English.
你总说我语法很标准
even when I stumbled,
even when I knew
you meant:
比我好。
I used to correct your articles
the hospital, not *a*.
You nodded, eyes already
on the next item.
Now, when my students speak,
I hear your pauses.
How their mouths wrap
around words, asking for permission.
一个男孩问我：
Is 'will' the same as 'going to'?
I want to explain
tense, aspect, certainty.
Instead, I say:
Yes.
I remember
You sitting by my beside,
说："我现在做梦都用英文。"
Then you asked,
"这是好事吗？"
I didn't answer.

18

I was thirteen.
Trying not to become you.
Now I text you in English.
你回：*吃了吗?*
Then:
Don't forget jacket. Very cold.
My students write essays
about 雪, about 外婆,
about the quiet between syllables.
They scratch out what they mean
and replace it
with what they think they're allowed.
I try not to teach them
what I learned from you
how to apologize
for speaking.
Sometimes I tell them
about a woman
who named her son 胜利,
Victory,
because passing English
was the last test.
They nod and understand her.
Sometimes I think,
你要的不是语法，
it's grace.
Some days,
I think I've learned
to speak
like you.

Allison Zhang

Mother Tongue with No Mouth

In the cave of my throat
live all the women I've been—
wolf-lunged, ox-shouldered,
braided into the spine of some ancient beast
who forgot her own name
but not the scream it carried.
They chant when I sleep,
those daughter-gods of salt and thunder,
filling my ears with wind,
my dreams with rivers
that don't end at the sea,
but circle back to the wound.
My first word was a crow
scratching at the roof of my mouth.
My second, a thunderclap.
They punished me
for speaking in storm
so I learned to whisper in rain.
I was born under a rusted bell
beside a mother who named me
for the ox that wouldn't kneel.
She fed me fire,
said I was built
from the bones of a forgotten shrine.
They carved grammar into my back
with reed and ash.
Told me it was language.
Told me it was survival.
But I knew:
it was a tether.
Still I rose—antlered,
muzzled in flame.
It is lonely to be a myth

in a world full of men.
To be prayed to
only when they are desperate.
I am what returns
when you call the wrong name.
Not ghost. Not god.
But the in-between. The horned dusk.
The last wind before winter.
If I ever return to the maker,
may I arrive
all fang, all hoove, all hymn—
an offering they do not dare refuse.
Let the final word be
untranslated.
Let it bloom with teeth.

Allison Zhang

A Fictional Portrait of Immigrant Fluency

WHEN I GOT HOME, the ceiling was already speaking again—
small throat-clears of footsteps, the ones from the neighbor above
who walked like he'd just been born and hadn't figured out
balance yet. Baba sat on the kitchen floor with the dictionary
open like a prayer book, his fingers tracing each word as if they
might come alive and bow back. He didn't notice me at first. The
dictionary was one of those fat ones with a broken spine and
green duct tape, the kind the school library was trying to throw
out until I took it home. I liked it better than the online ones. You
could hear the rustle of progress.

"You're back," Baba said, looking up without lifting his head.
"Today I learn fifteen new words. You want to test me?"

Before I could answer, he held up a finger like a stop sign. "Wait. I
forget. Let me rehearse again. Then test." He returned to
mumbling softly, repeating "affection, affection, affection," like it
was a command. I didn't tell him that no one used that word out
loud anymore unless they were reading a letter from 1943.

The kitchen floor was cold but Baba said it helped keep the words
inside his body, so they wouldn't evaporate through his pores.
Sometimes he taped flashcards to his chest like armor. Other
times, he made me quiz him while we watched TV, and if he got
it wrong, he punished the remote. It wasn't violent—just a stern
lecture into the batteries. "You see? I am not stupid. I am practicing. Practicing means you still believe there's time."

~

In our apartment, the walls were made of air and disappointment.
You could hear other families loving each other louder. Our
family loved in lowercase, in leftovers. In "are you full?" and "you
need jacket?" and in the fact that Baba always unplugged the

microwave after using it, as if saving the house from some slow electrical death.

There were three clocks in our home, but all of them ticked differently. Baba said this was a metaphor for our immigration. I said maybe the batteries just needed changing. He laughed. "See? Fluent already."

∾

Once, Baba told me the story of how he learned the word *errand*.

"You know," he said, "in China, it just means go do something small. But here, everyone say it with such power. 'I have to run *errands*.' So important. Like king business."

When he worked as a janitor, the office manager once asked him if he could run an errand. Baba said, "I don't run. I mop." They laughed. But he didn't.

After that, he practiced. "I am running an errand. I am an errand runner. I am runner of errands." He muttered it on the bus, at stoplights, even once during a dentist appointment, which made the hygienist pause her scraping and say, "Excuse me?"

Now every Sunday, he goes on a ceremonial walk and comes back with things we didn't ask for—milk, string, sometimes a single glove—and calls it an *errand*.

∾

He believed English had a shape, like a body, and if you could hold it right, it wouldn't slip. At night, I would find him speaking to the mirror, sculpting his mouth into foreign vowels like he was molding dumplings. But dumplings are soft. These words had bones.

I remember one morning he asked, "Why school never put me in ESL when we come?"

I shrugged. "They thought you didn't need it."

He tapped his head. "But needing is not seeing. They think if you don't fall, you're fine. But I fall inside."

~

In his free time, Baba wrote poems in a notebook he called "my fluency dreams." I read one once. It said:

"Language is a city.

I came in the back gate.

I don't have the map,

but I carry the sound of my mother

like a key."

The apartment smells of ginger and ink. Baba uses the back of takeout menus to write down irregular verbs. The television hums, waiting for attention. A page turns. He looks up.

"Test me," he says again.

So I do. I say, "Affection." And he closes his eyes. Smiles. Says, "My daughter."

Dear Mother, Dear Father

Last night I lit the candle you left
in the drawer beside the rice.
The wick caught slowly,
I watched the flame move
not up, but around.
Soft as breath learning to stay.
Do you remember the storm that took out the lights?
How we sat in the kitchen,
faces lit from below,
the wax pooling like milk?
You called it temporary.
I thought you meant the darkness.
Now I think you meant the light.
When I speak English,
it feels like that flame
held in a room that doesn't belong to me.
But it stays.
Some days I say the wrong thing.
I watch people blink.
Still, I stay in the room.
Still, I keep the candle lit.
I know I can describe this—
but I only know it in your language.
And when I try to say it out loud,
it disappears in the throat.

Allison Zhang

I write to tell you
the candle is almost gone.
But the wax remembers heat.
And I do too.
With love,
Your daughter
(still learning how to hold a flame)

Now They're Saying Place Is a Kind of Memory

The vine keeps growing where
the wall forgets to say no.
You mistake the stain for water
until it grows into handwriting.
Some words change form
when spoken in warm air.
You said your name once
and the echo chose a different version.
A courtyard doesn't wait;
it keeps time in moss.
The doorway bends, the paint
lifting like breath held too long.
Above the window, characters
watch without translation.
You want to believe the past
can still hold its ink.
A landscape painting in your living room
unfolds into something breathing.
That shape in the corner—
you once thought it was you.
Your father said it wasn't
but looked away too slowly.
Now the real tree leans
just enough to question its shadow.
You keep your hands in your pockets,
think they might still carry the right weight.
The wind shifts, and for a moment
you understand what wasn't meant.

Allison Zhang

Dear House,

*I'm back & / you didn't wait for me. / The swing still yawns from
one hinge / & the paint peels.*

*The stairs don't recognize me. / I step & they flinch. / The hallway
blinks / as if light were a rumor / someone told too late.*

*I reached for the switch / the way I used to / elbow, flick, hope / but
the bulb sputtered / then nothing. / a tongue twisted tight / after too
many years / of no one calling.*

*The kitchen smells / of burnt oil / & rain on metal. / Familiar, but
distant. / an accent worn thin.*

*I touched the wall / where we marked my height / each summer. /
Gone. / Painted over / or maybe erased / by time with nothing better
to do.*

*I sit on the floor / of the room where I first learned / to break my
name / into English. / Each syllable a scrape. / Each question / a
hallway I couldn't finish.*

*The window still opens / to the neighbor's fence / & the orange tree /
that once looked half-dead / is blooming now / late, but certain.*

Some things grow / by waiting.

Others forget / what they were reaching for.

You held my figure / but not my weight. / That's fair. / I left.

*Now I come back / with a suitcase that smells / like other places / & a
mouth that speaks / like it's been somewhere.*

So I guess / this is me / knocking.

Yours, /

or not anymore, /

—A.

The Language Between Us

On displacement from fluency

In the beginning, I only spoke when I had to. "Here," during roll call. "Bathroom?" when I couldn't hold it any longer. And "I don't know," which I said even when I did.

I learned English slowly, like walking into cold water. My classmates moved through it like fish. I stayed at the shallow end, memorizing textbook phrases that never came in time.

At home, we spoke Chinese. I did not know the word "immigrant," only that it meant we were starting over and the price was language. My mother would ask me to translate school emails, insurance letters, bank statements. I didn't always know the words, but I learned to guess.

When I got it wrong, she didn't blame me. She just said, "It's okay. Try again."

But I knew what it meant to be unsure in two languages.

On displacement from ease

In third grade, I stopped bringing my lunch to school. Not because I didn't like my mother's cooking, but because every time I opened my thermos, someone would ask what it was. "It smells weird," they'd say. I nodded and began throwing it away.

Later, my mother found the uneaten food and asked, carefully, if I didn't like it anymore.

"It's just... easier," I said.

She didn't ask again. After that, she packed sandwiches with Kraft singles and turkey slices. The bread was always slightly damp. I ate every bite.

Sometimes I think my mother learned English just to read labels, just to get the lunch right.

On displacement from clarity

At school, I translated her notes into cleaner English. Changed "My daughter no can come Monday" to "My daughter will be absent on Monday." Changed "I go with her to dentist" to "She has an appointment." I took out the parts that felt too raw.

Even now, I rewrite her texts before forwarding them to others.

I do it without thinking. Fix the verbs. Smooth the tone.

She has never asked me to.

On displacement from confidence

In high school, my English improved. I started writing essays that made teachers pause. They called it "lyrical." I didn't know what that meant, but I liked how it sounded.

Sometimes my mother would ask me to help her prepare for interviews. "You speak better," she said. "You know how to sound right."

We would sit at the kitchen table and practice. I asked questions I had heard before. "What are your strengths?" "Why do you want this job?"

She answered carefully, repeating my words until they stopped sounding foreign.

When she got rejected, she smiled as if it didn't matter.

But at night, I heard her listening to YouTube videos on pronunciation. I watched her mouth move silently, practicing.

On displacement from belonging

In public, people compliment my English. "Wow," they say, "you don't even have an accent."

I nod, like it's a prize. Like I'm not still translating myself in my head.

When people ask if I speak Chinese, I say yes, but not like a native speaker. Not anymore.

Between the two, I've learned to be fluent in nothing.

On displacement from family

At the DMV, I fill out forms for my mother. She signs without reading.

On the phone, I pretend to be her. "Yes, this is she," I say, mimicking her clipped tone. I have memorized her birthday, her Social Security number, her medical history.

She jokes that I know more about her than she does. I laugh. But I don't correct her.

On displacement from time

At a parent-teacher conference in fifth grade, a teacher said I was "not participating enough." My mother apologized. "She shy," she explained. "But she try hard."

That night, I sat on the floor with a list of English idioms and tried to memorize them like flashcards. "Break a leg." "Piece of cake." "Hit the books."

My mother sat next to me, nodding along, repeating the ones she could remember. "Break a leg," she said, and smiled. "We learn together."

I didn't know how to say it then, but I remember thinking: this is the only language that belongs to both of us now. Not perfect, not first, but shared.

On displacement from self

Now, when I write essays, I think of her. I think of the pauses between her words, the slight hesitations, the way she smiles after every sentence like she's checking to see if it landed.

When I speak in public, I borrow that rhythm. Not out of habit, but because it's the first voice I ever knew.

At home, we still mix languages. I speak to her in English. She answers in Chinese.

We understand everything.

On what remains

For her birthday, I pick out a card with simple words and write in smaller ones beneath them. I add the sentence: "Thank you for everything you've taught me."

She doesn't say much. Just holds the card for a long time, fingers pressed to the corners.

There is no perfect phrase for what we have. But we are still speaking.

Still reaching.

Still here.

The Lost Language
It isn't discussed enough how English language learners lose their native languages in the process of learning English.

Edge of the Sea

The stones of the sea are like many, many heads.
They want to marry us, the hands are waves.
We lie down on a blue-that-isn't-blue blanket,
I bought it at the end of the world—very cheap.
The waves take pictures of us, like paparazzi.
Families come out, grow like flowers,
open umbrellas, coolers,
children run into air that tastes like salt, like crying.
I know words are not enough, my love.
The seagulls already start to sing their desire,
it's not a song, it's hunger, it's wanting.
They will all get what they want,
and the sea will sing until night begins to dance.
I said before: I don't want to marry.
I was young. I wore clothes that weren't mine,
my mother's clothes, too big.
The years ate me, little by little.
But now, the river's mouth is a star.
The sun rides our backs, like a cowboy.
You are sleeping, belly shining with oil
from cheese, crackers, soft beer.
Music glows behind us.
I've never felt this warm.

Allison Zhang

Borde del Mar

Las piedras del mar, son como muchas muchas cabezas.
Ellas quieren casarse con nosotros, las manos son olas.
Nosotros estamos acostados, en una manta azul-que-no-es-
azul,
la compré al final del mundo—muy barata.
Las olas toman foto de nosotros, como paparazzi.
Familias salen, crecen como flores,
abren paraguas, hieleras,
niños corren al aire que tiene sabor a sal, como lloro.
Yo sé palabras no son suficiente, mi amor.
Las gaviotas ya empiezan a cantar su deseo,
no es canción, es hambre, es querer.
Todas van a tener lo que quieren,
y el mar canta hasta la noche empieza a bailar.
Yo dije antes: no quiero casar.
Era joven. Usaba ropa que no era mía,
ropa de mamá, muy grande.
Años me comieron, poquito a poquito.
Pero ahora, la boca del río es estrella.
El sol monta nuestras espaldas, como vaquero.
Tú estás dormido, barriga brilla con aceite
de quesos, galletas, cerveza suave.
Música brilla atrás.
Nunca he estado tan calientita.

海边

海里的石头，好像很多很多头。
它们想跟我们结婚，手就是浪。
我们躺在一块不是蓝的蓝色毯子上，
我在世界尽头买的——很便宜。
浪在拍我们照片，像狗仔队。
一家一家出来了，像花一样长出来，
打开伞，打开冰箱，
小孩子跑进空气，空气有咸味，像哭。
我知道，亲爱的，语言不够用。
海鸥已经开始唱它们的想要，
不是歌，是饿，是渴望。
它们都会得到它们要的，
海唱到晚上开始跳舞。
我以前说：我不想结婚。
那时我很年轻。穿的衣服不是我选的，
是妈妈的，太大了。
这些年，一点一点把我吃掉。
但现在，河口是明星。
太阳骑在我们背上，像牛仔。
你睡着了，肚子亮亮的，
都是奶酪、饼干、轻酒的油。
音乐在我们后面发光。
我从来没这样温暖过。

What slips between tongues can still shimmer like salt.

place and displacement

"No two languages are ever sufficiently similar to be considered as representing the same social reality."– Edward Sapir

Edward Sapir

Three Women in Transit

MAIN STREET—FLUSHING, NY

I took the train north after missing my transfer twice. The woman at the station said the platform had changed. I didn't understand her at first, thought she said "perform." I asked her to repeat, and she spoke slower, louder, as if my hearing were broken instead of my fluency. I nodded, smiled, and thanked her anyway. I had been fluent once. In Mexico, I gave speeches. I told jokes. Here, the jokes tell themselves. I watch them pass by on subway ads, missing the punchlines. I rehearsed what to say if asked for my ticket. Then said nothing when asked. Just showed it, already crumpled, in the wrong hand. I stayed with a cousin I hadn't seen in ten years. Her apartment smelled like dried squid and laundry sheets. She asked if I still spoke "like that." I said no. I didn't say I missed it. The way language felt loose and fast in my mouth. Here, I speak like I'm pulling teeth from stone. I carry a notebook where I write down words I don't know. *Invoice. Persimmon. Appropriate.* Once I asked someone what "ambiguous" meant, and he said, "You know—like this moment." At night, I watched the city from her fire escape. Tried to count how many windows flickered blue. Below, sirens folded into the rustle of leaves. I heard a man on the phone shouting *You never listen, you never listen,* and thought he might be right, even if he wasn't talking to me. The neighbor's child said hi when I came back inside. I answered too slowly. She looked up at me and asked, "Do you talk weird because you're new?" I told her I'd been here a while. She said, "But you still sound like that." Later, I washed my face in the cramped bathroom and saw someone had written *YOU ARE NOT YOUR ACCENT* on the mirror in dry-erase marker, fading. I didn't know if it was meant for me. I wiped it away with my sleeve. The next morning, I practiced saying "good morning" before anyone was awake. It came out as an apology.

Astoria, NY

I moved into a sublet above a halal butcher. The walls smelled faintly of lamb fat and bleach. My roommate left notes on the fridge in English—*don't leave rice in the cooker overnight, buy more toilet paper*—and signed them all with smiley faces, as if that softened anything. I translated them twice, just to be sure. I answered only once. She didn't ask again. The laundromat was five blocks away. The first time I walked there, I tried to memorize the machines' instructions. I pretended to read quickly. Watched what the others did. Counted coins carefully before slipping them in. I didn't know how to ask for change when I ran out, so I bought a pack of gum at the corner store, paid with a ten, and said nothing. The cashier looked at me too long, then dropped the bills into my open palm, like I was a child. I listened to podcasts in English while folding shirts. *Today on Radiolab...* The voices were too fast, but I let them fill the silence. I believed if I just listened enough, something would come back. In Chengdu, I gave directions to tourists. Here, I walk with my phone open, rerouting every block, always slightly lost. The butcher downstairs plays the same song every morning, something slow and mournful in a language I don't know. I look it up sometimes, find nothing. I imagine the lyrics mean *I have arrived* or *I miss my mother.* The day it rained, I sat by the window and watched the pigeons huddle under the scaffolding. One had a limp. It moved strangely, but with purpose. I thought of my father then. His walk, his quiet. His way of fixing things without speaking. That evening, a boy on the street stopped me to ask for directions in Spanish. I answered in English, slowly. He smiled, nodded, and said *thank you,* like it mattered. For a moment, I didn't feel foreign. Back upstairs, my roommate had left another note: *Dinner's in the fridge if you want.* No smiley face. Just steam rising off the rice, the smell of ginger and garlic, and the hum of the fridge. Something is finally beginning to thaw.

Allison Zhang

Greyhound Bus, I-80

I boarded in Reno at dusk. The driver didn't check my name, only
scanned my phone, said *back row's free.* I took a window seat near
the bathroom. A man across the aisle spoke into his phone in low
bursts, then fell asleep with it still in his hand. His ringtone was
Twist and Shout. When it went off again at 3 a.m., no one looked
up. The speaker above me buzzed with static. I listened for station
names, understood only fragments. *Elko. Salt Lake. Layover.* I
kept the ticket stub in my pocket and touched it every hour, a
proof of passage. Maybe if I held it long enough, I'd become
someone who belonged in motion. A woman got on in
Winnemucca and sat beside me. Her coat smelled like tobacco and
peppermint. She asked where I was from, and I said, *California.*
She raised her eyebrows. I added, *Before that, El Salvador.* She
nodded, then said nothing. We rode without speaking for six
hours. She offered me half her sandwich. I said thank you and ate
it slowly, chewing each bite like it might be a word I'd forgotten.
Somewhere past Salt Flats, we hit snow. The world outside went
white, but the windows fogged too quickly to see. I watched my
own reflection as I practiced a phrase for the job interview: *I'm a
quick learner. I'm good with systems.* It sounded hollow, too clean,
something taken from someone else's mouth. At the next rest
stop, I bought a cup of watery coffee. The clerk said *Have a good
one* and I replied *You, too,* except it came out slanted. A delay
before the *too.* He tilted his head, then turned to the next
customer. I poured three sugars into the cup and took it back to
the bus, still hot in my hands. Just before dawn, the woman
beside me tapped my shoulder and whispered, *You talk in your
sleep.* I asked what I said. She shrugged. *Something like not now,
maybe later.* I didn't ask which language. I already knew it wasn't
English.

After Words
A Fictional Short Story in Four Voices

~

Jessica
(Paraguay → São Paulo → New Jersey)

The first time I raised my hand in English class, I thought my voice would betray me. Not the words; I practiced those. It was the vowels, the breath between them, that I worried would sound foreign.

But I said, "May I read?" and the teacher smiled like I'd offered her something delicate. I was fourteen and already knew how to make myself small.

At lunch, I sit with the girls who don't laugh loudly. We open our Tupperware and unwrap our languages like paper napkins: quiet, necessary. Reem's Arabic is fast and soft, which I like to think of as falling water. Mei's Cantonese sounds clipped and musical.

When they speak English, their voices tilt upward at the ends of sentences. I try not to do that. I want to sound sure.

I used to write poems in Portuguese. Now I translate them, syllable by syllable, until they bleed out on the page. It's like trying to transplant a tree using only tweezers.

Reem
(Aleppo → Amman → New Jersey)

People here ask where I'm from, thinking of it as a riddle. I give them the answer, but they don't really want it. "Oh," they say, and their eyes do the rest.

I like numbers more than words. Math doesn't get offended when I mispronounce it.

Still, I come to Ms. Rivera's class because it's one of the only places where no one rushes me. She lets me write comics instead of paragraphs. I draw girls who say everything I can't.

Jessica is good at talking. I don't think she realizes that. She always knows the words for things. When we read aloud in class, I listen to the way she drops her consonants like she were born here.

Sometimes I wish I could steal someone else's voice, just for an hour. Not forever—just to know what it's like not to be asked, "Could you repeat that?"

Mei

(Hong Kong → Vancouver → New Jersey)

I memorize words while other girls memorize boys.

"Ephemeral."

"Indelible."

"Effervescent."

Beautiful syllables that sound like they float.

I came here last year. At first, I didn't speak much—not because I didn't know how, but because I didn't know if anyone would wait long enough to listen.

I miss reading fast. In Hong Kong, I used to win speech competitions. Now, when I read aloud, I scan ahead so I don't trip over the long words.

Jessica and Reem are the closest thing I have to a lunch table I belong to.

We don't match. We don't talk all the time. But when I say something complicated, Jessica nods like it made sense. When I say I forgot how to say something in English, Reem fills in the blank without making it a big deal.

That's all I want. A space where I'm understood before I'm corrected.

Amy
(Shandong → New Jersey)

I watch my mother rehearse phrases in English before she calls the pharmacy. "Hello. My name is... I need to pick up..." She murmurs them, even when no one's listening.

Maybe that's why I keep a list of things I want to say but haven't. I write them down in my journal, then underline them, hoping that maybe one day they'll sound natural:

—"That's not what I meant."

—"I disagree."

—"Let me finish."

At school, I don't speak much unless I'm sure the sentence will survive.

Still, I've started answering questions in class. Not fluently. Not beautifully. But clearly.

Ms. Rivera says my writing has a voice. I don't know what that means yet.

In Table 3, we don't say everything. But we say enough.

We say "try this," and "me too," and "you're getting better."

That's something, more than I could have ever hoped for.

UNDERSTOOD
A Play Based on the Life of Marisol Vargas

SCENE 1. FIRST WORDS
STAGE LIGHTS UP:

INT. ELEMENTARY SCHOOL CLASSROOM – DAY
(A second-grade classroom buzzing with activity. Children draw pictures with crayons. The teacher, MS. HENDERSON, tapes up vocabulary cards: apple, book, desk, window.)

MARISOL AS NARRATOR (V.O.)
(adult Marisol)
The first word I ever spoke in English was "bathroom." I had practiced it for a week. Ba-th-room. Two syllables. No R in Spanish like that one. I waited until I had to pee so bad I was crying. Then I raised my hand.

YOUNG MARISOL (7) *sits at her desk, legs bouncing under the table. She raises her hand timidly.*
Bathroom?

(MS. HENDERSON gives her a thumbs up. Marisol runs out, clutching a hall pass.)

MARISOL AS NARRATOR (V.O.)
That was my first win. A thumbs-up and an empty bladder.

SCENE 2. MAMI'S HOUSE
INT. SMALL APARTMENT KITCHEN – EVENING
(MAMI cooks arroz con pollo. The scent fills the tight

44

kitchen. A Spanish soap opera plays low in the background.
MARISOL (now 10) does homework at the table.)

MAMI
(accented, gently)
¿Tú necesitas ayuda, mija?

YOUNG MARISOL
No, está bien.
(She pauses.)
Mami... what's a... what do you call it ... metaphor?

MAMI
(pulls a chair, sits)
It's when you say one thing, but mean something else.
Like when I say you're my whole heart. You are not liter-
ally my heart. But you are.

MARISOL AS NARRATOR (V.O.)
I didn't understand metaphors in English. But I lived
them every day in Spanish.

SCENE 3. PARENT NIGHT
INT. SCHOOL CAFETERIA – NIGHT
Posters for "Back to School Night" hang on the walls.
MARISOL walks beside MAMI, who wears her nicest
blouse and heels. They sit across from MS. HENDERSON.

MS. HENDERSON
Marisol's doing very well in reading. A little quiet. But
very smart.

MAMI
(nods, smiles tightly.)
Thank you... teacher. *(halting)*

MARISOL AS NARRATOR (V.O.)
I translated the rest. I was eight years old, and already the
bridge between two worlds. My mother was smart too.
Just not in the language Ms. Henderson measured.

SCENE 4. THE TEST
INT. STANDARDIZED TESTING ROOM – DAY
*(Students sit spaced apart. YOUNG MARISOL stares at a
bubble sheet.)*

MARISOL AS NARRATOR (V.O.)
The questions weren't hard. The words were. Words like
"seldom," "benevolent," "meticulous." I knew their
cousins in Spanish. But cousins don't always speak to each
other.
*(Marisol bubbles an answer. She chews her pencil. A BOY
behind her whispers something cruel in English. She doesn't
respond.)*

MARISOL AS NARRATOR (V.O.)
Some people thought I was slow because I was quiet. But
quiet isn't stupid. Quiet is translating every word before
you dare speak it out loud.

SCENE 5. LOCKER ROOM
**INT. MIDDLE SCHOOL LOCKER ROOM –
AFTERNOON**
*GIRLS laugh and shout. MARISOL (now 13) fumbles
with her locker. A WHITE GIRL eyes her.*

WHITE GIRL
Your English is good.
(pause)
Do you dream in Spanish or English?

MARISOL
Both.

WHITE GIRL
That's so cool. I barely passed Spanish class. Say something in Spanish.

MARISOL AS NARRATOR (V.O.)
People like hearing Spanish when it's entertainment. Not when it's real.

MARISOL
Yo no soy tu show.

WHITE GIRL
What?

MARISOL
(nods, softly)
Exactly.

SCENE 6. ABUELA'S STORY
INT. ABUELA'S LIVING ROOM – NIGHT
ABUELA sits in a rocking chair. MARISOL sits at her feet with a notebook.

ABUELA (IN SPANISH)
Cuando llegamos aquí, no sabía cómo decir leche, pan, o gracias. Pero todavía comimos. Todavía vivimos. Y tú, mija, vas a volar más lejos que todos nosotros.

(Marisol writes. The words come out half in English, half in Spanish.)

MARISOL AS NARRATOR (V.O.)
I didn't know then I'd be a writer one day. That language, even in fragments, could still be whole.

SCENE 7. ORAL PRESENTATION
INT. HIGH SCHOOL CLASSROOM – DAY
MARISOL (now 16) stands at the front of class, holding note cards.

MARISOL
Growing up bilingual means I have two homes in my mouth. Some days, English is the house I'm still building. Other days, it's Spanish that feels like the one with cracks in the walls.
(Students are silent. One kid claps. Then more.)

MARISOL AS NARRATOR (V.O.)
It took years to say I was proud. But it's true now. I carry two languages. And neither one is broken.

SCENE 8. FULL CIRCLE
INT. ELEMENTARY SCHOOL CLASSROOM – PRESENT DAY
MARISOL (early 30s) is now the teacher. She kneels beside a nervous little girl.

LITTLE GIRL
(in Spanish)
No entiendo.

MARISOL
(softly, kindly)

Está bien. I'll help you. Little by little, okay?
The girl nods.

MARISOL AS NARRATOR (V.O.)
This time, I'm the one who understands. And I know
exactly what to say.

LIGHTS FADE OUT

THE END

MOUTHFUL

The first word Terrie ever learned in English was "milk," but she didn't say it out loud until two months later, when her tongue no longer felt like a foreign object in her mouth. By then, the cafeteria milk had already gone lukewarm.

She told no one it was her favorite word. She liked the soft click of the "k," the way it ended quickly and politely, unlike the words she used at home that dragged their feet across her teeth.

That winter, the school gave her a speech therapist. She thought it was a punishment. The woman's office smelled like lemon Lysol and dry glue. The woman made her say words into a mirror. *Ship. Sheep. Pitch. Peach.* She stared at her own face as it mouthed foreign sounds. She started to dream in syllables that had no meaning, just shape.

Her mother cleaned houses. Sometimes she came home with the smell of other people's soap on her clothes, or a bruised banana in her coat pocket. She would hand it to the girl wordlessly. They barely spoke anymore, not in the language they both knew, not in the one they were supposed to be learning.

The girl spent her evenings in the closet under the stairs. It wasn't because she was scared, but rather because it was the only place that didn't echo. She lined the closet with her old notebooks, walls coated in loops of imperfect cursive, as if to trap her voice inside. Her teachers called her quiet. "Shy," they said, when really she just didn't trust her mouth yet.

Once, she tried to explain "hunger" to her ESL tutor. Not the kind you get at lunchtime. The kind that sits behind your ribs. The kind that speaks with no voice. Her tutor nodded and said, "You mean motivation." But that wasn't the word. That wasn't it at all.

❧

The boy across the hall from her lived in a glassy apartment full of bright rectangles. He had an electric toothbrush that hummed at the same pitch every morning, a blue backpack with patches stitched by someone who loved him. He liked to wave at her through the peephole in the laundry room door. Sometimes he offered her gum and said the flavors slowly so she could pick: *peppermint. cinnamon. spearmint.*

He called her "M," even though her name was not an M name. She didn't correct him. She liked the structure of it—how it started in the lips. He gave her a book once: *A Wrinkle in Time.* She couldn't finish it because she kept stopping at the words she liked best: *tesseract, wrinkle, shadow.*

One night, when the hallway lights flickered and the floor smelled like bleach, she found the boy crying beside the vending machine. His backpack lay open beside him like a dead animal. She didn't know what to say. So she just sat down next to him and offered him a piece of gum.

He said, "My mom left again."

She said, "Me too."

Neither of them asked what the other meant.

❧

In her dreams, her voice came back. But it looked like an animal. Long and dark and low to the ground. It followed her through parking lots and train stations and empty stairwells. In one dream, she fed it alphabet soup and it refused to eat the vowels. In another, it spoke in a voice that wasn't hers—older, broken, with the wrong accent.

She started keeping words in her mouth during class. Just to see how they tasted. Some were like coins. Others like ash. She could feel when a word belonged. It had weight. Warmth.

There was one word she never spoke aloud: *feral.* She found it in a book about wolves. The description said: "undomesticated, wild, reverting to a primal state." She wrote it five times in the margins of her planner. The letters looked like claws.

She wasn't wild. She brushed her hair every morning. She said *excuse me* in grocery store aisles. But she understood the word anyway.

~

The school put her in a debate class to "build confidence." One day, they gave her a prompt: *Should immigrants assimilate?* She had to look up the word "assimilate." She wrote it on a post-it note and folded it three times until the paper became a hard pellet. She didn't speak the whole debate.

Her teacher said she had potential. That was another word she disliked. It always felt like a warning. Like the air before thunder.

~

She never said *I love you* in English. Only in her first language. That one had more teeth in it. It felt riskier. But true.

Years later, someone would ask her how she learned to speak so clearly. She would shrug. But in her head, she would remember:

- The way milk sounds soft.

- The boy in the hallway with the broken backpack.

- The animal in her dreams.

- The gum that tasted like peppermint.

- The closet under the stairs.

- The word she never said.

She would think about how language doesn't arrive like a light switch. It leaks in. Like water, smoke, the scent of something warm, cooking in a house where no one has spoken in hours.

And still—

you know someone is home.

school, silence, and systems

"Do you know what a foreign accent is? It's a sign of bravery."

Amy Chua

Allison Zhang

What We Google Instead of Ask

Group Chat: "Friday Crew 🍕"

Miguel is a high school student who recently moved from El Salvador. At home, he speaks only Spanish with his parents, while learning to navigate English at school and with friends.

LIA: soo are we still doing movie night or what
• •

JORDAN: yes pls i need smth chill after this week 😩

RINA: i'm down

but only if someone else brings snacks this time lol

MIGUEL: i can go

what time?

LIA: around 7ish

we'll see lol

JORDAN: don't pull a last time Miguel 😵 😵

RINA: yeah you showed up halfway thru the movie 💀

MIGUEL: haha yeah

my bad

i'll be on time

LIA: "on time" but for real this time

MIGUEL: yes

like 7? or

a little before?

RINA: honestly we just hang for a bit first

u good

MIGUEL: ok

i'll be there

Miguel puts his phone down, then picks it back up. Opens Google. Types: "we just hang before movie meaning." Closes the tab without clicking anything.

JORDAN: bring those chips again if u can

MIGUEL: i'll try

not sure if store has

LIA:anything's good tbh

just don't bring raisins like jordan did that one time 💀 💀 💀

JORDAN: wow

i'm being attacked

MIGUEL: raisins are good

but ok 😒

He stares at the chat. Wonders: "What time does it actually start?" Doesn't ask. Decides to show up at 6:45, just in case.

Allison Zhang

Group Chat: "APUSH Gang 🔥"

Ana is a high school student who recently moved from Colombia and is still learning English

> RILEY: FYI the DBQ for APUSH is due ASAP or Ms. T's gonna go MIA again 💀 💀
>
> JAMES: lol she really said "your grade is your problem" 😭
>
> KELSEY: ASAP???
>
> she just assigned it tuesday bruh

> ANA: yea
>
> i remember
>
> she said that
>
> crazy 😭

> RILEY: yup
>
> so like finish it today or risk it
>
> also FAFSA deadline's next week yall don't forget

> ANA: yeaa
>
> i do it
>
> almost done

Ana stares at the screen. Types: "fasa meaning school" in Google. Sees results. Still unsure.

> ANA: i think i saw it in email
>
> or somewhere
>
> too many stuff lately lol

KELSEY:

same

my inbox got like 300 things rn

20 seconds pass. Ana re-reads everything. Her heart kind of sinks.

ANA: btw

the dbq

is like

with the sources?

or no

RILEY: yea with docs

u gotta cite at least 3

and do contextualization and all that

ANA:

ah

ok

thx

She stops typing. Doesn't really know what "contextualization" means. Doesn't want to ask. Tries to move on.

ANA: i try to finish soon

if not today then

tonight maybe

RILEY: cool cool

send it to me if u wanna check it

ANA: ok

ty

1 minute passes. Ana switches apps, copies all the acronyms into Notes. Types under them: "check what these mean later." Then back to chat.

ANA: wait

srry

what is

the MIA

RILEY: oh lol

it just means she won't be at school tomorrow

ANA: ohhh

i see

i thought was like

another form or test

RILEY: nah just slang lol

you good

ANA: k

just checking

Search History (Private Window)

how to pronounce "rural" without sounding stupid
can you lose accent by practicing
why do americans talk so fast
how to say "i don't understand" without looking dumb
ESL phrases to sound more fluent
how to join conversation without interrupting
why do people laugh when i talk
what does "never mind" actually mean
difference between "excuse me" and "sorry"
how to say no without being rude
what to do if teacher skips your name during attendance
how to make friends in english
how to stop translating in head
when does accent go away
how to order food without panic
how to say "i miss you" without crying
english words for when you feel small
can you dream in a second language
how to say "enough" without raising voice
how to talk like you belong
how to explain your parents don't speak english
how to ask for help without feeling ashamed
how to sound normal
how to sound normal
how to sound like me

Search History
(Mother's Phone, Nighttime, After Homework)

what is past tense of eat
why teacher call my daughter "resilient"
how to say "you can do it" in good english
meaning of "fluency" in school
english words for proud but quiet
can a child be translator for parent
how to write email to teacher without mistake
what is IEP
what is honor roll
what does "college track" mean
how to say i love you without sound weak
what does "you're doing amazing" mean
how to ask for help nicely
why my child speak english but not chinese
how to teach heritage language
how to say "i miss talking to you"
how to not be problem at school
how to understand school letter
how to say "i'm trying"
how to understand my daughter's jokes
what does "you wouldn't get it" mean
how to say "i'm proud" so he believes me
how to say "i'm still your mother"
how to keep up
how to catch up
how to not fall behind

Search History
(Father's Phone, Nighttime, After Work)

how to help child with school projects without perfect english
what to pack for field trip when school gives no list
how to say "i'm proud of you" so it doesn't sound soft
why does daughter correct my pronunciation
how to read between lines in teacher comments
meaning of "high expectations" in american schools
can i join parent meeting if i don't speak well
how to ask principal for interpreter without making trouble
what is "growth mindset" exactly
why daughter speak different at home and outside
how to help with essays when i only know simple words
how to know if child lonely at school
what is "subtle" when people say humor is subtle
english phrases that sound confident
how to answer school email with respect
what is "AP class" and is it good
what to say when daughter says "you don't understand"
how to keep first language alive at home
how to not embarrass child in front of classmates
can school punish if parent makes mistake in form
how to support dreams i don't understand
how to explain i'm learning too
what does "dad you're doing fine" really mean
how to ask for second chance without sounding weak
how to stop feeling left behind
how to be good father in new language

Allison Zhang

Borderline

as a child of two tongues
I learned to measure silence by the minute
I wanted to say
look at me
not
look at my score
I sat in the back
of the gifted testing room
with a translator who didn't come
& when the proctor spoke too fast
I nodded
because confusion is softer than shame
in my youth
where English cracked like glass
in my mouth
I started to hear the rumors
he can't keep up
she's delayed
they're behind
delay:
they called it that
as if language were a bus
that came late
only for children like me
never mind that I could solve
every puzzle in math class
before the instructions finished
but not in the language they gave me
referral
is the nice word they used
before they sent me down the hall
to the "other" room
the one with fewer books

fewer futures
they said
this is support
this is help
but it felt like
a closed door
with my name scratched out in pencil
my mother cried
when they told her
I didn't qualify for the gifted program
"he just needs more time," she said
in a language they didn't bother to hear
I was not behind
I was bilingual
but no one saw that as brilliance
just burden
I was not confused
I was translating
every single thing
from the roll call
to the lunch form
to the humiliation
they say
giftedness is potential
but only if your potential
sounds like theirs
why do they test our worth
in a language we're still surviving?
why do they punish accent
& call it data?
if I flinch now
when someone asks
"where are you from"
it is not fear
it is memory

of what they took
when they labeled me wrong
of the classrooms I never entered
of the gifts they never opened
how far is the line
between silence and sabotage?
how many of us
buried our brilliance
just to pass?
today
I speak in full
& fluent
anger
but once
I was only a child
who wanted to say:
I am not slow.
I am learning.
I am not behind.
I am bilingual.
I am not broken.
You just weren't listening.

The Listener's Notes

Marginalia from an Imagined Educator

I first heard of the Listener from one of my grandmother's old students—a woman named Ladan who now taught ESL at a community center in Sunset Park. We were sitting on folding chairs in the back of a church basement, and she was explaining why she refused to give grammar tests.

"The Listener taught me," she said.

"Who?"

"You've never heard of him?"

"No."

"Then you haven't read the right textbooks."

That night, I went back to the garage and rummaged through the rest of my grandmother's papers. Buried in a pile of annotated syllabi was a copy of *Language for Beginners* by Miriam Goldman. The spine was cracked, the margins overflowing with notes not in my grandmother's handwriting but in another script—looser, slanted, as though written in motion.

Every so often, the words "—Kr." followed the note. I came to think of it not as an abbreviation, but a signature. Kr. The Listener.

Page 37: The Simple Present Tense

(The exercise: Match the subject to the correct verb.)

Marginalia: *They already know how to match. What they need is to matter. Let them speak about things they love. Use the grammar to catch them, not cage them. —Kr.*

I started dreaming about him shortly after that. In the dreams, he stood at the whiteboard of a flickering classroom, chalk in one hand, a comic book in the other.

"Comprehension is not a test," he said in one dream. "It's a breath. A beat. A moment where the words mean something real."

He drew a large input funnel on the board.

"i+1 is not a formula. It's a whisper of something just barely out of reach. The best teachers don't drag the learner toward it. They drift beside them until they arrive."

When I woke, my hand hurt from writing. I looked at my night-stand and found a piece of paper I hadn't remembered scrawling on. Three words:

Input is invitation.

Page 59: Irregular Verbs

(The activity: Fill in the blank using "went" or "gone.")

Marginalia: *Let them get it "wrong." Wrong is warm. Wrong is alive. You didn't teach your child to speak by correcting their every sentence. You smiled, and they spoke more.* —Kr.

I asked Ladan again if the Listener had ever published anything.

"No. He doesn't believe in books," she said.

"Then how do we learn from him?"

"You listen. That's the point."

"To what?"

"To what they're trying to say before they know how to say it."

I became obsessed. I started to think maybe Krashen—Stephen Krashen, the linguist, the theorist, the man behind the Input

Hypothesis—was just the first version of him. The Listener is what he became after he passed through academia and into story.

"Let them read," the Listener said in another dream, "but don't assign it. Let the pages fall into their hands like rain."

Page 86: Classroom Conversation Starters

(Prompt: What did you do last weekend?)

Marginalia: *Stop asking them what they did. Ask them what they dreamed. Ask them who they miss. Ask them what their grandmother's voice sounds like in their language. That is English too.* — Kr.

Sometimes I think the Listener isn't real. That Krashen never wrote in the margins of old textbooks, and that Ladan invented him just to make me feel something when the data stopped meaning anything.

But other times, I think the Listener is everywhere—in the corner of every classroom where the quietest student waits, in the mouths of children who translate for their parents in grocery stores, in the pages of the library books no one signs out but everyone reads.

And I remember what I read in the final note, tucked between pages 109 and 110:

You do not need to be corrected to be understood. You need to be listened to. I am always listening. —Kr.

Allison Zhang

From TRANSLATION

Five lamplight halos drown in the parking lot.
A boy mouths the word elevator like prayer.
Something mechanical rises anyway.
Who taught him to conjugate
without a body?
His pencil traces circles instead of tenses.
In the cafeteria, steam speaks louder
than any voice he recognizes.
Tray, orange, milk, the word try.
Behind the glass, a flag waits.
The counselor says just say it how you think it should sound.
He says it, how he thinks,
and they laugh.
Why laugh? Why have you come here?
A teacher whispers you are doing great
but the boy doesn't know
if great means pass
or disappear.
Maybe language
was a door.
Maybe someone forgot to tell him
it only opens one way.
The dictionary on his desk
has fifty-seven words for stop.
Only one for home.
Somewhere, a buzzer sounds.
Somewhere, a sentence ends
without its subject.

You Ask Me If I Mind Working Alone
after Maggie Smith

I don't. But you ask again,
like maybe this time I will.
What would I want instead?
A name written next to mine.
Not much else. Not noise,
not the scratching of too many pens.
I want someone asking
what I think before I graduate.
A chair already pulled out.
A page passed toward me, not over.
On second thought, nothing passed.
Only room to speak and be heard.
You ask if I'm fine.
I nod, and keep the answer small.

Allison Zhang

I Speak for Them

TITLE: I Speak for Them
Scene 1: After the Meeting

SETTING
Back parking lot of Lindale Elementary School. Winter coats on chain-link fences. Security light flickering. Mop bucket wheels squeak somewhere offstage. Wind. Trash. A school banner hangs sideways on the fence: *Every Student, Every Voice.*

CHARACTERS
MS. ELENA CORTEZ, 38, ELL teacher. Steady, sharp, constantly balancing exhaustion and restraint.
MRS. JOAN RICKERT, 53, PTA president. Polished, smiling, surgically passive-aggressive.
MR. CHAD DOYLE, 46, district administrator. Thinks he's progressive because he's nice to custodians.

(*Lights up. MS. CORTEZ stands stage left, coat half-zipped, holding a closed thermos. She's staring out at nothing. MRS. RICKERT enters in heels that don't belong on cracked concrete.*)

MRS. RICKERT
You're still here.

MS. CORTEZ
Car battery's dead. Or dying. Not sure yet.

MRS. RICKERT
Want a jump?

MS. CORTEZ
No jumper cables.
(*Beat.*)

MRS. RICKERT
You were... passionate in there.

MS. CORTEZ
Is that a compliment or a warning?

MRS. RICKERT
It's an observation. You're always so... fired up.

MS. CORTEZ
I'll try to be less noticeable next time. Maybe speak through a PowerPoint. With animations.
(*MR. DOYLE enters, holding a Starbucks cup and the minutes from the meeting. He's already texting.*)

MR. DOYLE
Evening, Elena. You made an impact tonight.

MS. CORTEZ
Did I? I must've missed it while you were budgeting us out of existence.

MR. DOYLE
No one's being cut.

MS. CORTEZ
No, just restructured. I know. You're very careful with the verbs.

MRS. RICKERT
Let's not turn this into a thing.

MS. CORTEZ
It *is* a thing, Joan. I spent the last three weeks prepping sixteen ELL kids for a reading benchmark written at a tenth-grade level. One of them has been here five months. He still says "blanket" when he means "thank you."

MR. DOYLE
But he *knows* the word blanket. That's a start.

MS. CORTEZ
It's not the same thing.

MRS. RICKERT
You act like you're the only teacher who cares.

MS. CORTEZ
I'm the only one expected to be an interpreter, therapist, truancy officer, and grammar mechanic in one prep period.

MR. DOYLE
That's not entirely accurate.

MS. CORTEZ
Then come sit in. Watch how often they ask if their parents will get in trouble if they write the wrong thing. (*MR. DOYLE looks down, suddenly busy with his phone.*)

MRS. RICKERT
You're personalizing this too much.

MS. CORTEZ
They're kids. It *is* personal.

MR. DOYLE
(half-joking)
Here we go.

MS. CORTEZ
You know, I spent the whole meeting trying to figure out how many of the board members even knew what ELL stands for.

MRS. RICKERT
English Language Learners.

MS. CORTEZ
Right. And how many of them know that when funding gets cut, it doesn't just mean fewer books. It means Diego doesn't get help when he starts writing backwards again. It means I don't have time to call Lina's mom when she stops showing up.

MR. DOYLE
You're assuming a lot of responsibility.

MS. CORTEZ
Yeah. I noticed.

MRS. RICKERT
Elena. I understand your frustration—

MS. CORTEZ
Do you?

MRS. RICKERT
I have three kids.

MS. CORTEZ
Do they translate letters from immigration for their parents?
(*Beat.*)

MRS. RICKERT
That's not the point.

MS. CORTEZ
Then what is? That we're all underfunded, so I should shut up and take the hit quietly?

MR. DOYLE
You could try working with us, instead of always being—

MS. CORTEZ
Always being what? Angry? Difficult?

MRS. RICKERT
Uncompromising.

MS. CORTEZ
I'm not compromising a kid's future so the robotics team can have matching hoodies.

MR. DOYLE
You're not the only one who cares.

MS. CORTEZ
No. I'm just the only one who has to say this out loud every year like it's news.
(*She pulls a crumpled worksheet from her bag. Hands it to Doyle.*)

MS. CORTEZ
This is from Noor. She's seven. She wrote, "I live in a big bag with my brother." We think she meant *bus*. Or *van*. Doesn't matter. I asked her if it had windows and she said yes, but they're broken.
(*They don't look at the paper.*)

MS. CORTEZ *(CONT'D)*
But sure. Let's reallocate.
(*Long beat. Wind picks up. Something blows across the stage. None of them move.*)

MRS. RICKERT
It's not like we don't want to help.

MS. CORTEZ
You just don't want to help at a cost.
(*Her phone buzzes. She checks it. Pockets it.*)

MS. CORTEZ *(CONT'D)*
That's Marco's mom. She's stuck at her second job. Asked if I can walk him home.

MR. DOYLE
That's not in your job description.

MS. CORTEZ
No. But apparently none of this is.
(*She finally sips from the thermos. It's cold. She doesn't react.*)

BLACKOUT.

reclamation and power

"Language is not neutral. It is a means of inscribing power."

Bell Hooks, Teaching to Transgress

Allison Zhang

Repeat After Me

"Repeat after me."

I already did, in my head.
But it sounded different when you said it.
"No—say it with confidence."

My voice isn't broken.
It's just shy from being punished.
"You have to try harder."

I stay up past midnight translating every word.
Even the ones that hurt.
"We can't understand you."

That makes two of us.
"Let me say it again, slower."

I know what the words mean.
I just can't make them sound like you.
"Is this how you talk at home?"

Home has more than one language.
None of them ask me to prove myself.
"Don't be afraid to make mistakes."

I made one the first time I opened my mouth here.
And you laughed.
"I'm just trying to help."

Help should not feel like shrinking.
Should not sound like "fix."
"You'll get better with practice."

Echoes and Entrances

I know someone who spoke seven languages.
None of them made her fluent in being heard.
"Say it again. From the top."

Again, again, again—
until I disappear beneath the sentence.

Allison Zhang

Tonguework
for every kid who got laughed at reading aloud

My English came second—
like the second plate at the table.
The one you didn't ask for
but still needed to feel full.
My grandma called it
the ugly tongue.
Said it twisted too much.
Sounded like soap and fear.
Tasted of someone else's country.
But still—
I worked it.
Back of class.
Back of throat.
Reading Holes out loud
like the words had teeth
& I was learning
how not to bleed.
The W's made me stumble.
The Th's—
knocked my tongue sideways.
Even now,
I say "think" like "sink."
And maybe that's truer anyway.
My father said,
"If you talk like that,
no one's gonna hire you."
I said,
"What's dumber than silence?"
This mouth?
It holds leftovers.
It holds my mother yelling
through boiling water.

82

It holds prayer.
& curse.
& the names they gave me
before I could spell them.
This accent—
ain't broken.
It's bruised.
And still
it sings.
It's cassette tape gospel.
It's karaoke in the wrong key.
It's messy.
It's loud.
It's mine.
I don't need perfect
to speak holy.
I need breath.
And a little room.
So here—
take this sentence.
Try to laugh.
But know:
Every time I mispronounce something,
I'm building a country
that still says yes
to me.

Allison Zhang

"The Word for Smoke"

LUIS SAT at the desk in the narrow room, writing slowly. He was trying to finish the last sentence of a scholarship essay—something about perseverance. He hated that word. It felt like something adults said after the worst part was already over.

I persevere because...

The sentence stalled there, heavy. The word *because* pulsed on the page, deciding whether to live.

Outside, the wind stirred the jacaranda branches. A crow screeched. Luis looked up, startled, then back at the paper. The deadline was at midnight. The scholarship was for "students overcoming linguistic adversity." He wasn't sure what counted. Was it when the cashier pretended not to hear him? Or when he answered correctly in class but everyone laughed at the way he said *phenomenon*?

His mother was asleep in the next room, the low static of a telenovela humming through the wall. He thought about waking her, asking how to say *overcome* in Spanish. But the word felt stiff when translated. Like it had to pass through too many hands before reaching him.

The lamp flickered once.

He blinked. Then something happened.

The words on the page loosened.

Persevere uncoiled from the line and rose like steam.

Because broke apart, each letter spinning gently in the air.

Luis froze. The words hovered, weightless.

Then, one by one, they fell into his open palm, warm, as if they had been spoken first.

He looked down. Ash on his skin.

The page was clean again.

He picked up the pen.

I kept going. That's enough.

And he hit submit.

Allison Zhang

Mouthfeel

S-s-say it.
Th. Thh. Thhhh.
Tongue between teeth.
Not Tuh. Not Duh.
But like a soft punch.
Like whispering thunder into a cup.
I say tree
when I mean three.
Say it again.
Three.
I bite air.
Teacher nods like prayer.
World gets stuck in my throat.
Wor.
Werrrr.
Wuh-rld.
A rolling stone
that never settles in my mouth.
I practice in bathroom mirrors.
Face becomes echo.
I mouth: February
like a wound I want to close.
Feb-roo-wary.
Feb-yoo-airy.
Forget it. Just say "second month."
Comfortable feels like
chewing socks.
Comef-ta-bull?
Cumfturble?
Why make words
no one wants to say right?
"Excuse me."
"Sorry."

"Sorry."
"Sorry."
The easiest word.
Always ready.
Soft on the tongue.
Heavy on the back.
My mouth is a crowded hallway.
Too many sounds
walking past each other
without eye contact.
They say "Repeat after me."
But English echoes wrong.
Like running in shoes
meant for someone else.
Still
I speak.
I spit vowels like seeds.
Consonants cut.
R's drag.
Still
I speak.
And maybe
this is the most fluent
I'll ever be.

Allison Zhang

The Polyglot's Testament

An Unearthed Manuscript on Language and the Displaced

In the summer of 2024, just a few months before I was set to defend my dissertation on semantic shifts in English as a Second Language (ESL) instruction, I discovered a glowing USB drive hidden inside a hollowed-out copy of *Woe Is I* on a dusty shelf in my grandmother's garage in Flushing, Queens. My grandmother, who had taught ESL for thirty years in New York City public schools, had died that spring, and I'd returned to help my cousin Minh sort through her books, worksheets, and what she called her "teaching relics"—old vocabulary posters, broken cassette players, coffee-stained lesson plans from the Clinton administration.

I only opened the book because it fell on my foot. The USB, when plugged into my laptop, displayed a single file: The Polyglot's Testament.docx. The first line stunned me.

I, E. Linh, eternal learner and transcriber of language's secret rivers, leave this record for those who whisper in accent, who stutter toward belonging.

The writing was archaic, fluid, uncanny. But what caught my attention most was the script—not Times New Roman, not Courier. The text was rendered in what appeared to be a living font, the letters shifting subtly depending on the viewer's mother tongue. When my cousin Minh read it, the first paragraph rearranged itself into Vietnamese-inflected English. When I opened it, it smelled faintly of the chalkboards from my childhood ESL classroom in P.S. 13.

I was a scholar of second language acquisition, specifically morphosyntactic flexibility in heritage learners, and I had never seen anything like this.

There is no one English, only echoes. I once taught in the school between realms, where children spoke in ellipses and teachers

88

corrected dreams. Each student arrived with a suitcase of syllables and tried to exchange them for citizenship.

That's when I realized what I might be reading: the lost memoir of E. Linh, a mythological figure in ESL lore, rumored to have written the first curriculum that taught English to birds. Legend said Linh had once conducted a parent-teacher conference entirely in sighs and metaphors, and that her students had gone on to become poets, politicians, subway announcers, even Alexa.

When I was eleven, my grandmother told me a story about Linh slipping into a standardized testing facility and rearranging the answer bubbles so ELL students could pass by intuition alone. I had laughed, thinking she was joking.

Now I wasn't so sure.

As I read further, the document revealed itself as part diary, part spellbook, part pedagogy. A random entry:

April 3rd: Javier conjugated the past perfect of "to dream" as "I had dreamt of home." I did not correct him. It was too beautiful. The grammar of migration is not always tidy.

Another:

May 19th: I taught silence today. Had each student bring in the sound of their mother's voice saying their name. We transcribed the pauses. Cecilia's pause was five seconds long. She cried afterward and said it felt like writing in her first language again.

It was all too surreal. I emailed my advisor, the TESOL International Association, and Noam Chomsky. No reply.

The next section of the manuscript was titled "The Glossary of the Untranslatable." Each entry described a word that no language could fully hold:

- Graccent (n.): The melody of one's origin laced into the consonants of a new language.

- Unvoice (v.): To be talked over in a classroom where your words arrive one second too late.

- Whispwrite (v.): To write an essay with the fear that someone will read it and laugh.

- Lingerrain (n.): The dream of fluency carried in the pockets of people who've forgotten their childhood tongue.

Toward the end of the manuscript, the tone shifted. Linh had begun traveling—not in the world, but in syntax.

I moved into the subjunctive mood today. It's a place with no gravity. "If I were fluent" drifts through the air. Children build homes out of hypotheticals.

And then, the final entry:

I leave now. My students no longer need me. I've folded myself into a phrasal verb. Tell them to look for me in the margins, in the comma splices, in the red pen's mercy. I will be there.

I closed my laptop. My throat felt tight. Outside, the Q27 screeched past the house.

Later that week, I returned to Columbia and handed in my dissertation: "Syntax of the Sacred: Mythos and Pedagogy in the Teaching of English to the Displaced." I included selections from the Polyglot's Testament as an appendix. My committee didn't know what to make of it. One professor called it "a compelling fiction." Another accused me of forgery.

No matter. I had read Linh's final line.

Echoes and Entrances

There is no native speaker of belonging.

And I believed it.

Allison Zhang

Underpainting

You tilt your head
as I speak. A small motion.
Enough to feel it.
The lamp behind you flickers
like a mistake I'm afraid to make.
We are in a room that could be
anywhere—Amsterdam,
or just a second-floor apartment
with the window shut.
You smile
when I say the word wrong.
Throat. It becomes something
between thought and thread.
You say it back to me, gently,
as if correcting
a painting.
Vermeer used ultramarine
in shadows,
not where it was supposed to go.
Blue where the eye
least expected it.
My voice
is full of those shadows—
colors mined from elsewhere,
sent here to glimmer quietly.
At home,
my name means river.
Here, it is shortened,
smoothed, something
you can say
without asking.
In your mouth,
I become almost fluent.

You don't know how much
I practice disappearing.
Vermeer painted women reading
letters they would never send.
I mouth whole stories
before answering Yes, I understand.
What you hear
is the finished surface.
What I carry
is underpainting:
the teacher who sighed
when I paused,
my mother who said
"speak louder,"
as if volume
was the only border.
Still—
you hand me your phone,
ask me to translate
a message.
And for a moment,
I am the one
who knows.
In the silence that follows,
you don't ask
where I'm from.
You only say
my name—
the full one.
As if
it fits.

part two

preface

For as long as I can remember, I've been fascinated not only by the personal experiences of English language learners (ELLs) but also by the legal and social forces that shape our education. Part II of this book explores how systemic changes in law, policy, and public perception have impacted ELL students in the United States. I wrote the following essays to provide context for the challenges ELLs face today—from landmark court cases like *Lau v. Nichols*, to classroom realities like standardized testing and bilingual education. Understanding this history matters because it shows how our voices, as students and community members, can help drive change. This is my attempt to bridge the personal and the political, giving readers a clearer picture of why the ELL journey looks the way it does, and what still needs to improve.

voice as systemic change

(History of English language learners and Current Problems They Face)

Struggles and Successes of *Lau v. Nichols* (1974):
The Supreme Court Decision that Revised English Language
Learner Education

ON JANUARY 21, 1974, the Supreme Court issued a decision in
Lau v. Nichols (1974) that would significantly alter the education
of English language learners (ELLs)—"students who are unable to
communicate fluently or learn effectively in English"—in the
United States.* Indeed, Lau v. Nichols is often cited as the landmark case that established ELL educational rights.†

However, the immediate aftermath of the decision brought significant uncertainty. Legislative pushback and social backlash
quickly weakened its execution. Despite these repercussions, the
Court's determination sparked immediate action toward giving
ELL students linguistically accessible resources, including bilingual education. This case also initiated research that gradually
shifted schools toward bilingual education, benefiting ELL
students over time.

A few months before January of 1974, seven Chinese ELL
students, one of them Kinney Kinmon Lau, along with their
parents, initiated *Nichols*.‡ They first brought a class suit to the
District Court because they believed that the San Francisco
Unified School District (SFUSD), represented by SFUSD
President Alan H. Nichols, violated the Fourteenth
Amendment.§ This amendment states that "no State shall make
or enforce any law which shall abridge the privileges or immuni-

---

* "English-Language Learner," *The Glossary of Education Reform*, last modified
May 14, 2014.
† Ileana Najarro, Timeline: The U.S. Supreme Court Case That Established
English Learners' Rights," *Education Week*, January 2024.
‡ "Lau v. Nichols," *Oyez*.
§ "Lau v. Nichols."

ties of citizens of the United States."* Specifically, the students addressed how the SFUSD failed to provide accommodations for ELL students, needed for them to learn at the same rate as native English speakers.† Therefore, the school district significantly hindered ELL students' learning ability, abridging their privileges to education.‡ After failing to win their case in the District Court and the Court of Appeals, the plaintiffs brought this case to the Supreme Court.§

The Supreme Court ultimately ruled that the SFUSD's ignorance of ELL students' needs, negatively affecting around 1,800 students, violated the Fourteenth Amendment and the Civil Rights Act of 1964, which bans discrimination based on national origin.# This court decision labeled language-based discrimination —not giving non-native English speakers the same opportunities as native English speakers—as a form of discrimination based on national origin. Thus, any school district that failed to provide ELL students with adequate language learning opportunities violated the Civil Rights Act of 1964.°

The court agreed with the plaintiffs that ELL students faced severe disadvantages because all the classes required learning material in English, which these students did not know enough to understand.** Therefore, even if ELL students had the same textbooks, teachers, and curriculum as native English speakers, their inability to comprehend the material's language meant that they could not receive a meaningful education, violating the

---

* U.S. Const. amend. XIV, § 1.
† "Lau v. Nichols."
‡ "Lau v. Nichols."
§ Launch Nichols, *Beyond Brown: Launching the Legal Fight for School Desegregation*, PBS.
# U.S. Equal Employment Opportunity Commission (EEOC), "Title VII of the Civil Rights Act of 1964," last modified September 9, 2023.
° Leslie Villegas, "The State of Language Rights and Bilingual Education 50 Years After Lau v. Nichols," *New America,* Last modified January 14, 2023.
** "Lau v. Nichols."

Fourteenth Amendment.* This finding emphasized that school districts must give these students language-appropriate resources to ensure a thorough understanding of the course material. This ruling also supported bilingual education, a relatively unknown program at the time, but which could resolve language barriers through classes taught in both English and students' native languages.†

Following this case, legal repercussions undermined its enforcement, as the Supreme Court decided on cases that the community then directly used to weaken the precedent of *Nichols*. Thus, the Supreme Court inadvertently made decisions that hurt *Nichols'* enforcement power. For instance, eight years after 1974, *Guardians Ass'n v. Civil Service Commission* (1982) occurred.‡ During this Supreme Court case, Black and Hispanic police officers alleged that a civil service exam discriminatorily and disproportionately affected minority groups.§ This exam included multiple culturally biased questions tailored to the educational experiences of white people, creating a barrier to minority groups who didn't receive the same education because of systematic obstacles.# Although Title VI of the Civil Rights Act of 1964 protects against discrimination based on race and color, the Supreme Court ruled in favor of the city's policy to implement a civil service exam.° The court determined that the city had proved these exams as "job-related"; thus, these tests were necessary within the community. The Court reasoned that because the

---

* "Lau v. Nichols,"

† "Bilingual vs. ESL," *5 Minute English*.

‡ Guardians Association v. Civil Service Commission of City of New York, 463 N.Y.S.2d 45 (App. Div. 1983).

§ Guardians Association v. Civil Service Commission of City of New York, 1983.

Guardians Association v. Civil Service Commission of City of New York, 1983.

° U.S. Department of Housing and Urban Development, "Title VI of the Civil Rights Act of 1964."

exams were job-related, they could not be declared illegal—even if they produced discriminatory outcomes.[*]

Based on this decision in *Guardians,* the implementation of *Nichols* lost power. Many people drew a connection between the "job-related" and therefore required nature of civil service exams with the "job-related" and thus mandatory nature of public services like education.[†] Hence, even if a school district chose not to implement bilingual education and disproportionately affected ELL students, courts could not punish these districts for violating the law because they provided the essential education service. School districts took advantage of this decision to restrict bilingual education, as they faced little repercussions, and discouraged ELL students from fighting against districts that implemented unequal education. With this power imbalance between school districts and ELL students, the execution of *Nichols* became significantly weaker.

The power of implementing *Nichols* suffered further damage from *Alexander v. Sandoval* (2001), as this case clarified the limited ability of individuals to act under Title VI of the Civil Rights Act of 1964. During this Supreme Court case, the plaintiff Martha Sandoval challenged how Alabama's policy of only administering driver's license tests in English disparately impacted non-native English speakers.[‡] Sandoval's challenge brought into question whether private plaintiffs such as herself could sue for disparate impacts—the "adverse effect of a facially neutral law"— under Title VI.[§] The Supreme Court ruled that Title VI does not contain any private right of action to address disparate impact

---

[*] Guardians Association v. Civil Service Commission of City of New York, 1983.
[†] Rachel F. Moran, "Undone by Law: The Uncertain Legacy of Lau v. Nichols," *Berkeley La Raza Law Journal* 16 (1): 1–10, 2005.
[‡] "Alexander v. Sandoval," *Oyez.*
[§] Kimberly Amadeo, "Disparate Impact," *Investopedia*, last modified August 5, 2021.

discrimination; therefore, Sandoval had no right to sue Alabama for its policy having disparate impacts, only being able to do so if she could find that the state intentionally discriminated against a minority group.[*]

Because Sandoval clarified that Title VI offers no private right to sue for disparate impact—and because Nichols had not firmly established such a right—many concluded that individuals could not sue school districts for discriminatory educational policies unless they could prove intent.[†] However, the Fourteenth Amendment already provided the right to sue for intentional discrimination. By inadvertently limiting *Nichols* to the power already given under the Fourteenth Amendment, the Supreme Court decision of *Sandoval* largely neutralized the implementation of *Nichols*: ELL students still could not sue school districts' policies that might disproportionately affect them. Although students could still try to prove discriminatory intent, doing so required clear evidence that school districts deliberately sought to disadvantage ELLs—evidence often difficult to obtain. As a result, many schools overlooked ELL students' needs without consequences.

In addition to legislative fallout, the execution of *Nichols* suffered due to the vague language in its court opinion, which enabled social pushback. For instance, although the court deemed it necessary for education to be more inclusive of ELL's native languages, the opinion of *Nichols* stated that schools must take "affirmative steps" toward helping children with limited English knowledge.[‡] This language left much interpretation to the school boards, which had to determine what phrases like "affirmative steps" meant. Some believed that "affirmative steps" simply meant providing English as a Second Language (ESL) programs—

---

[*] Alexander v. Sandoval.
[†] Moran, 2005.
[‡] "Lau v. Nichols."

already-instated ELL classes solely focused on teaching and using English.* For instance, Secretary of Education T.H. Bell vocalized how he would stick to ESL programs and thus avoid bilingual education: "We will protect the rights of children who do not speak English well, but we will do so by permitting school districts to use any way that has proven to be successful."[†] Bell's statement echoed how many educators wanted to "protect the rights" of ELLs through ESL programs but avoided bilingual education, which had yet to be explored and could not be "proven to be successful." On the other hand, others believed that affirmative steps meant going beyond ESL learning, even if that meant exploring new and under-researched methods. Raul Yzaguirre, President of the National Council of Hispanic advocacy group La Raza, said, "Bilingual education is the only really effective way to deal with linguistically different children."[‡] Those like Yzaguire thought schools should take affirmative steps by creating bilingual programs rather than sticking to ESL programs because ESL programs were ineffective for many ELL students. Others debated whether these affirmative steps should be temporary or sustained over time. With this breadth of interpretation in multiple areas of the case, many schools stuck to the traditional route and did not revise their educational systems.[§]

Even if people determined that *Nichols* sought to create bilingual education, many school districts opposed this finding because they worried that the number of ELL students was insufficient compared to the impracticality of implementing bilingual programs. This concern ultimately hindered the implementation of the Nichols decision. In Washington County, for example,

---

* "Bilingual vs. ESL," *5 Minute English*.

[†] Christopher Connell, "Axing of bilingual program raises Hispanic Fears," *Trenton Evening Times* (Trenton, New Jersey), February 8, 1981: 102, *NewsBank: America's Historical Newspapers*.

[‡] Connell, February 8, 1981.

[§] Villegas, last modified January 14, 2023.

most school districts contained a small number of ELL students.[*]
Even if one Washington school district had many ELL students,
they would usually be "spread out over 20 different schools and
12 grades."[†] Given this low number, implementing bilingual
programs seemed disproportionately costly and logistically difficult. Indeed, these programs often required a cost of around one
hundred fifty to three hundred dollars per student, a significant
amount when considered together.[‡] Bilingual education costs
more than an only-English curriculum because it requires buying
extra, language-modified resources and hiring bilingual teachers.
Yet, during the 1980s, the United States notably lacked Asian and
Middle Eastern teachers who could speak both English and their
native languages.[§] This deficiency meant school districts struggled
to find enough teachers for the diverse student population. Due
to high costs and a shortage of qualified bilingual teachers, many
districts concluded that implementing such programs was not
worthwhile given the small number of students who would bene-
fit. As a result, many schools failed to implement bilingual
programs despite the ruling.

On top of school districts not utilizing bilingual learning for practical reasons, many people also believed that this education would
harm students, diminishing the power of executing *Nichols*. Some
believed ELL students in these programs would miss key aspects
of American history and English language instruction.[#] Because
students in bilingual programs might miss key knowledge covered
in mainstream curricula, many believed that bilingual education

[*]   Ann Jansen, "Schools take wait-and-see stance on bilingual education,"
Oregonian (Portland, Oregon), December 30, 1980: 23, *NewsBank: America's
Historical Newspapers.*
[†]   Jansen, December 30, 1980.
[‡]   Polly Carpenter Huffman and Martha Samulon, "Case Studies of Delivery and
Cost of Bilingual Education, *The U.S. Department of Education,* April 1981.
[§]   Jansen, December 30, 1980.
[#]   "Spanish," *Kansas City Star* (Kansas City, Missouri), December 14, 1980: 140,
NewsBank: America's Historical Newspapers.

would create a dichotomy among U.S. citizens. Indeed, James J. Kilpatrick—an American journalist and author—wrote in 1980 that dual-language policies, when pushed too far, would be "bound to divide our people, to foster bloc and faction, and to raise linguistic barriers among us."[*] His concerns reverberated in the minds of many others, creating a fear of implementing bilingual education and, thus, hindering the progress of its application. Because of the lack of research, many U.S. citizens also believed bilingual education would be less effective than ESL programs: they thought that students retaining their native language while learning English would hinder their progress in developing English proficiency.[†] This negative belief in bilingual education caused many school districts not to follow the decision of *Nichols*.

Although *Nichols* suffered this legal and social backlash, the decision immediately improved ELL students' educational experiences. This change stemmed from the Supreme Court decision that providing ELL students with the same facilities and curriculum as native English speakers was inherently unequal.[‡] Consequently, many people began investigating their school systems to determine whether or not they provided language-accommodated learning for ELL students.[§] During these investigations, many discovered that schools lacked the proper assessments and textbooks for ELL students, as these students had to learn from the same materials and curricula as native-English

---

[*] James Kilpatrick, "Grave error to carry bilingualism too far," *Bellingham Herald* (Bellingham, Washington), August 11, 1980: 10. *NewsBank: America's Historical Newspapers*.
[†] Jansen, December 30, 1980.
[‡] James Kilpatrick, "Bilingualism: a good cause is pushed to bad extremes," *Evening News* (San Jose, California), September 8, 1980: 33, *NewsBank: America's Historical Newspapers*.
[§] Mary Ann Zehr, "Examining the Impact of Lau v. Nichols," *Education Week*, November 14, 2007.

speakers.* These discoveries triggered efforts of redress, with new organizations and advocates arising. For instance, the National Association of Bilingual Education (NABE) started in 1975, emphasizing educational equity and excellence for multilingual students.† This organization especially placed weight on maintaining students' native languages and cultures while learning English.‡ Moreover, many advocates like Stephen D. Krashen—an American linguist and researcher—stressed the importance of adequate resources and proper strategies for teaching ELL students, distinct from those for native English speakers.§ All these activists and organizations, of which many still exist today, pushed school districts to address the inequalities of resources found in ELL education. Thus, the U.S. democracy developed in that, while it had significantly disregarded the distinctive needs of ELLs beforehand, it began to place more weight on helping these students attain a more thorough and effective education.

As people started vocalizing their concerns over the deficient resources, many also began emphasizing the importance of bilingual education in order for ELL students to have equal education to native English speakers. Previously, minimal bilingual programs existed in the United States.# If, in rare cases, schools did have dual-language education, they implemented it as a mode of transition into English-dominant classes.° However, *Nichols* directly elucidated how public schools needed to address ELL students and ordered San Francisco schools to institute remedial

* Zehr, November 14, 2007.
† National Association for Bilingual Education, "NABE's Mission."
‡ National Association for Bilingual Education.
§ Stephen Krashen, "Tell the Truth: The Impact of High-Stakes Testing on Language Learners," *Books and Articles by Stephen D Krashen,* February 7, 2004.
# Zaidee Stavely, "Q&A: How the 50-year-old case that transformed English learner education began," *EdSource,* March 15, 2024.
° "Bilingual Education: A Critique," In *Immigration and Multiculturalism: Essential Primary Sources,* edited by K. Lee Lerner, Brenda Wilmoth Lerner, and Adrienne Wilmoth Lerner, 398-401, Detroit, MI: Gale, 2006, *Gale In Context: Global Issues.*

108

efforts, allowing students to "fully participate."[*] Many people took this Supreme Court decision as a marker that bilingual education played a prominent role for ELL students to participate fully. With this consensus sparked from state to state, the decision of *Nichols* increased bilingual education nationwide. This increase especially spiked in the 1980s, during which many Spanish speakers and others immigrated to the United States.[†] In 1980, the U.S. government spread $167 million among states for implementing these programs, allowing an estimated 300,000 children to participate.[‡] On top of the federal budget, the Los Angeles government spent $46 million on dual-language programs from 1979 to 1980, amounting to 4% of its total operating budget.[§] This financial support caused bilingual education to shift from transitional to mainstream classes, transforming many school districts' previous systems and curricula. This change happened rapidly—only a few years after the Supreme Court decision—but it significantly changed U.S. democracy by bringing forth the previously overlooked concept of bilingual education.

Not only did *Nichols* impact students in the short term, but it also had tremendous impacts in the long run, one of them being the concrete determination of dual-language education as an effective learning method for ELL students. After *Nichols,* many researchers became interested in bilingual education, which had previously received little attention before the Court's 1974 ruling. Consequently, these researchers began investigating the benefits

---

[*] Lerner, 2006.
[†] Joyce Gregory Wyels, "Bilingual Education," In *Immigration and Migration: In Context*, edited by Thomas Riggs and Kathleen J. Edgar, 83-88, In Context Series. Vol. 1. Farmington Hills, MI: Gale, 2018, *Gale In Context: Global Issues.*
[‡] Kilpatrick, August 11, 1980.
[§] Willliam Trombley, "Bilingual Education System Under Fire," *Omaha World-Herald* (Omaha, Nebraska), October 1, 1980: 32, *NewsBank: America's Historical Newspapers.*

and harms of bilingual programs.[*] Through various studies, researchers debunked the earlier myths that this education harmed ELL students. In 2006, Francis DJ found that dual-language programs improve long-term English reading and testing outcomes.[†] Lindholm-Leary and colleagues reinforced this finding through a 2013 assessment of ELL children that those enrolled in bilingual learning scored higher on standard English proficiency tests than those in mainstream English programs.[‡] Moreover, Montanari S. found in the same year as Leary that children developed strong English and Italian literacy skills despite a class being instructed primarily in Italian.[§] All these findings elucidated that bilingual education benefited ELL students, a concept still recognized today.

Moreover, simultaneously with their research about bilingual education, many researchers also began investigating whether or not ESL programs outweighed bilingual programs. They did so because if one outweighed another, school districts could change their curriculum to implement more of the beneficial program. Through this research, many discovered information that contradicted previous beliefs about ESL education's greater effectiveness than bilingual programs. A 2006 study of the effects of Proposition 227—a California ballot passed in 1998 that largely eliminated multilingual education in favor of ESL learning—found that restrictive language policies such as Proposition 227

[*] Leslie Villegas, "The State of Language Rights and Bilingual Education 50 Years After Lau v. Nichols," *New America,* Last modified January 14, 2023.
[†] Francis DJ, Lesaux N, August D, Language of Instruction, In: August D, Shanahan L, editors, "Developing Literacy in Second-language Learners," Mahwah, NJ: Lawrence Erlbaum; 2006. pp. 365–413.
[‡] Fred Genesee, Kathryn Lindholm-Leary, "The Education of English Language Learners," In: Harris K, Graham S, Urdan T, editors, *APA Handbook of Educational Psychology*, Washington, DC: APA Books; 2012, pp. 499–526.
[§] Simona Montanari, "A Case Study of Bi-literacy Development among Children Enrolled in an Italian–English Dual Language Program in Southern California," *International Journal of Bilingual Education and Bilingualism*, 2013;17:509–525.

were counterproductive.[*] Researchers attained this conclusion because a decade after the implementation of this proposition, ELL students still only had a 40% chance or less of becoming fluent in English.[†] The same occurred in Massachusetts, where, after restricting bilingual learning, grade retention, dropouts, and suspensions increased for ELL students.[‡] By elucidating the ineffectiveness and even harm of ESL programs, *Nichols* reshaped many people's previous beliefs that ESL programs were superior to bilingual education.

As a result of this research, support for bilingual education grew, leading to program expansions in multiple states. This shift built on the momentum of the 1980s, transforming schools to include programs with half of the class taught in English and the other half in the students' native languages.[§] In 2013, Oregon awarded nearly $900,000 to develop dual-language programs.[#] Moreover, in 2016, Senator Ricardo Lara created Proposition 58, which repealed most of Proposition 227.[°] By doing so, he removed the mandate only to have ESL programs and enabled schools to implement bilingual learning. All these efforts significantly boosted ELL education, allowing students to receive a more thorough education in recent decades. These changes advanced U.S. democracy in that it became more inclusive, allowing students of different national and linguistic backgrounds to receive language-appropriate learning, pertinent for these students to fully learn English.

---

[*] Ellen Goldenberg and Steven Wagner, "Reviving an American Tradition," *American Educator* 39, no. 3 (Fall 2015).
[†] Goldenberg, 2015.
[‡] Miren Uriarte, Nicole Lavan, Nicole Agusti, et al., "English Learners in Boston Public Schools: Enrollment, Engagement and Academic Outcomes of Native Speakers of Cape Verdean Creole, Chinese Dialects, Haitian Creole, Spanish, and Vietnamese," *Gastón Institute Publications*, no. 130 (2009): 73.
[§] Wyels, 2018.
[#] Goldenberg, 2015.
[°] Goldenberg, 2015.

The implementation of Lau v. Nichols faced significant setbacks, as later rulings in Guardians and Sandoval inadvertently determined that students cannot sue school districts unless they have proved discriminatory intent. Moreover, many U.S. citizens viewed the decision of *Nichols* to implement bilingual education as impractical and harmful. Despite the initial backlash, *Nichols* brought much more attention to the needs of ELL students, such as the lack of adequate resources and the need for bilingual education. Consequently, many school districts have rearranged their curricula to better accommodate ELL students, leaving a lasting impact on the educational system of the U.S. democracy.

Yet, numerous challenges still exist for ELLs. These challenges include practical barriers, such as a lack of resources and teachers. Currently, textbook publishers hesitate to develop materials in non-English languages because of limited marketability and, thus, profit.[*] Without enough ELL materials on the market, schools either have to pay high prices or make do without these textbooks, damaging ELL students' learning experiences. Moreover, school districts still struggle to find enough bilingual teachers, particularly those with knowledge of Asian languages.[†] Because of this lack of teachers, many schools prematurely take students out of bilingual programs, having to make room for incoming students.[‡] Therefore, both factors—the deficiency in textbooks and teachers—directly harm ELL students' educations, as they do not receive adequate learning to become fluent in English.

Another challenge persists more abstractly: the U.S. culture surrounding ELLs. Though the U.S. has made progress since the 1980s, people still hold negative views of immigrants, many of

---

[*] IDRA, 2024.
[†] David Washburn, "California to Boost Number of Bilingual Teachers in Asian Languages," *EdSource*, March 24, 2022.
[‡] IDRA, 2024.

them ELL students.[*] For instance, in September of 2024, Donald Trump repeated a baseless claim of Haitian immigrants eating their pets—a stereotype stemming from xenophobia.[†] Comments like Trump's create a stressful learning environment for ELL students as they constantly have to watch their actions and words in case they further exacerbate a negative stereotype. This continuous stress, labeled as a "stereotype threat," causes ELL students to lose focus on their academics.[‡] Additionally, these harmful comments affect other students, who exclude ELL students based on these toxic stereotypes. Under an anxious and socially isolated learning environment, ELL students struggle with their academic performance, damaging their chances at language acquisition.[§] Thus, although *Nichols* has set a foundation of more effective learning opportunities for ELLs, much work remains to ensure that all ELL students receive the equal and accessible education they deserve. Only when these linguistic, legal, and cultural barriers are addressed will the promise of Lau v. Nichols be fully realized.

---

[*] Don Davis, "Poll: Half of Americans Support Mass Deportations of Illegal Immigrants," *Don Davis House*.
[†] Merlyn Thomas and Mike Wendling, "Trump Repeats Baseless Claim About Haitian Immigrants Eating Pets," *BBC News*, November 1, 2024.
[‡] Toni Schmader and Michael Johns, "Converging Evidence That Stereotype Threat Reduces Working Memory Capacity," *Journal of Personality and Social Psychology* 85, no. 3 (September 2003): 440–52.
[§] Stephanie Pappas, "How the Stress of Racism Affects Learning," *Association for Psychological Science*.

Bridging the Gap Between Educators and Families

When an ELL student approaches a teacher for help on a problem or something they need to change in the classroom, the result might be highly beneficial as the student voices their needs and allows a teacher to aid them. Moreover, this aid can also help the school, as one problem faced by an ELL might be encountered by many other students as well.

However, many ELLs are reluctant to take the initiative to speak to a teacher. This reluctance often stems from having a language barrier between the student and teacher, making it more difficult than it already is to approach a teacher or administrator for help. Without student feedback, schools struggle to adjust to best accommodate the students' needs.

Therefore, it is important to include family members in the school conversation, as ELL students are often more inclined to communicate with their families about the problems they face rather than administrators. Currently, there is a lack of this communication, mainly due to how educators or families can feel frustrated when talking to each other and not being able to understand one another. After a little while of this "failed" communication, most families stop trying to engage with the school, and vice versa.

Yet, the connection is vital, as "students with involved guardians often have better attendance, behavior, and grades." So, what can be done?

What has been done in the past—and is done quite often now—is asking students to translate or having another trusted person translate the information. Yet, this indirect method can still build up frustration, as "translators" can often miss out on crucial details and "bad" solutions, even if it is undoubtedly helpful in bridging the gap between educators and families. However, more long-term and beneficial solutions exist.

One of these solutions is to train current teachers to hold conversations in a foreign language simply. Although this method requires schools to put in more effort, it could have a "win-win" effect. On one hand, teachers can communicate with parents with minimal translation help; on the other hand, they can also increase student communication. For this to happen, many schools need to recognize the importance of family and educator communication and that simply sending notes to students' homes isn't enough, as it has to be an active conversation.

Another solution is to hire educators with insight into the student body demographic. For example, if the majority of the student body speaks Spanish, then it would be beneficial to turn attention to hiring bilingual teachers who are also fluent in Spanish. This method has the limitation of often being more costly, but it can greatly reward the school system, especially one with many ELLs.

If we want change in schools, we need to hear the voices of the students, including ELL students. To do so, it is pertinent that we bridge the gap between schools and families, creating a safe connection in which they can brainstorm solutions together.

Allison Zhang

Most ELLs Don't Only Face Struggles in English Classes

Often, English Language Learners (ELLs) are surprised to find that even though they're learning English in their language classes, their other subjects also require a strong command of the language. This can be frustrating for students who might otherwise succeed in classes like math or science if they were taught in their native language.

For example, math is often seen as a "universal" language, since it deals with numbers. But this idea overlooks a major factor: teachers explain problems in English, and word problems are written entirely in English. Many ELLs have trouble understanding instructions or test questions—not because they don't understand math, but because they don't yet have the English skills needed to make sense of the wording. As a result, ELLs tend to perform worse on academic assessments, even when they understand the core material.

One proposed solution is to have teachers teach in students' native languages. While this might be helpful in theory, it's often not possible in practice. Classrooms may include students who speak many different languages, making it difficult for a teacher to meet everyone's needs equally. Additionally, standardized tests are only offered in English. Without regular exposure to academic English in all subjects, students may continue to struggle on these exams.

Instead, teachers can use strategies that help students access content while also improving their English. One such method is the 3-Read Protocol. In this approach, students first read a word problem without any numbers so they can focus on understanding the language. Then, they read it again and try to predict what it might be asking. Finally, they read the full problem with numbers and work together to solve it. This process allows students to build confidence with the language before tackling the math.

Another strategy is to avoid long lectures. ELLs may not catch every word spoken in class. Providing visuals, like diagrams or examples, can help them understand the material without relying solely on verbal instruction. Teachers can also give students fill-in-the-blank activities to strengthen their vocabulary, giving them support while still encouraging active learning.

Flexibility is also key. Allowing students to occasionally use their native language when working through a difficult problem can make them feel more confident and engaged. Encouraging them to draw on their prior knowledge—whether or not it matches the U.S. curriculum—can help them find entry points into new material. Over time, their use of English will naturally increase as they gain confidence and skills.

It's completely normal for ELLs to struggle in subjects beyond English class. With the right tools and a willingness to adapt, teachers can support students as they grow. The most important thing is flexibility—giving students room to learn and recognizing that language and content learning can go hand in hand.

One Syllable at a Time: ELLs and Phonics

When native English speakers see the word *shake*, they often pronounce it without thinking. At some point in early literacy, though, they likely learned to separate the word into parts—*sh* and *ake*—before blending them. While fluent readers no longer rely on this process for familiar words, they still use it when sounding out unfamiliar ones. This skill, known as phonics, helps break the English language into approximately 44 distinct sounds, making it more manageable to learn. Rather than memorizing thousands of words, students learn to decode them by recognizing patterns in sound and spelling. Research confirms that phonics plays a foundational role in learning to read, starting with individual sounds and gradually building to full sentences and stories.

For English Language Learners (ELLs), the journey looks different. While native speakers begin phonics in kindergarten and often complete it by second grade, most ELLs start later, often with the added challenge of adjusting to a new language environment. Their first step is developing phonemic awareness, which refers to the ability to hear, identify, and manipulate the individual sounds in spoken words. This step is crucial because recognizing sound patterns in spoken English comes before recognizing them in written form.

Phonemic awareness can be especially difficult for ELLs. Many are still learning how English sounds differ from those in their home language. Some English words may look similar to words in other languages, but are pronounced very differently. Others contain sounds that don't exist at all in the student's native language. Without regular exposure and practice, it can be hard for students to distinguish these differences. Teachers can help by creating consistent opportunities for students to hear English in context. Reading aloud, repeating phrases, and singing simple songs can reinforce sound patterns. When students hear the same words multiple times, they begin to notice common vowel and conso-nant combinations.

Once students recognize these patterns, they can begin to apply phonics in their reading. One effective strategy is to have students match pictures to words. This visual connection reinforces vocab-ulary and allows teachers to check for understanding and offer feedback. These activities also keep learning engaging and interac-tive, especially for younger learners.

Even with a solid grasp of the 44 English sounds, ELLs often encounter irregularities. English doesn't always follow a consis-tent system of letter-to-sound correspondence. For example, the word *read* can be pronounced differently depending on the tense. Native speakers usually pick up on these shifts through repeated exposure, but ELLs often need more support. Teachers can help by pointing out these patterns explicitly and giving students opportunities to practice them in real-world reading and writing situations.

Learning phonics takes time, especially for ELLs who are navi-gating new sounds, spelling rules, and vocabulary all at once. To ease this process, teachers can introduce common sight words, such as *hello* or *goodbye*, that students can learn to recognize immediately. This allows students to save their energy for decoding new and more complex words using the phonics strate-gies they are developing.

In the end, teaching phonics to ELLs is not a one-size-fits-all task. Students come from diverse language backgrounds and will struggle with different words or sounds depending on their first language. Teachers must adapt their strategies, provide repetition, and offer consistent encouragement. Above all, they must recog-nize that acquiring phonics skills may take longer for ELLs, and that giving students the time and support they need is critical to helping them become confident, independent readers.

Allison Zhang

Standardized Testing for ELLs: Helpful, But Not Always Fair

Most students in the U.S. have taken standardized tests at some point, whether in elementary, middle, or high school. These tests became common after the No Child Left Behind Act (NCLB)was passed in 2002. The goal was to close achievement gaps by setting academic standards and measuring student progress. In 2015, the Every Student Succeeds Act (ESSA) replaced NCLB. ESSA still uses testing, but gives states more freedom to decide how to track success and support schools.

ESSA has brought some real improvements. It pushes schools to prepare students for college and helps low-performing schools by offering extra programs in reading and literacy. Since the law was passed, graduation rates across most states have gone up. Many schools now have rates above 80 percent, which is a big step forward.

Still, standardized tests don't always work well for English Language Learners (ELLs). These students already face the challenge of learning both a new language and new subjects at the same time. Testing adds another layer of difficulty. Many test questions use complex vocabulary or ideas that ELLs might not have fully learned yet, even if they understand the basic material.

Another issue is that the tests are all in English. This creates a problem, even in subjects like math. While math is supposed to be universal, word problems and instructions still require strong reading skills. That means ELLs might know how to solve a problem but struggle to understand what's being asked. This causes many to score lower in math, even if their math skills are just as strong as their peers'.

Some ELLs are also in bilingual programs, where they learn content in their home language while gradually transitioning to

English. These programs help students in the long term, but can make test scores look lower. That's because the test is in English, while the student may have learned the material in another language.

Newcomer ELLs—students who recently arrived in the U.S.—have even more to deal with. Standardized tests sometimes include questions about American culture or history. But if a student hasn't lived here long, they may not have learned that background. Even if they're doing well in class, they might still struggle on the test.

So what should schools do? Canceling tests for ELLs isn't the answer. Tests still matter, but the way they're given could change. For example, students could be allowed more time, or teachers could read directions out loud or help with translating instructions. That would give students a better chance to understand the questions and show what they've learned.

Another option is to make sure tests match what's actually taught in class. Test makers should avoid including tricky vocabulary or topics that weren't covered. Schools could also adjust their teaching to make sure students are ready for the kinds of questions that will be on the test. Either way, schools need to be part of the process and have a say in how the tests are written.

It's also important not to judge ELLs by the same exact standards as native English speakers. A test might not show everything a student has learned, especially if they're still building their language skills. Teachers should look at how students grow over time using smaller classroom assessments, not just one big exam. And when comparing schools, people should take into account whether a school has many ELLs, since those scores might look different even if the teaching is strong.

Tests should never define any student, and that's especially true for English learners. Yet, with a few changes, standardized tests can still be useful—but only if they're fair, flexible, and take each student's journey into account.

Understanding the Diversity of ELLs: Meeting Their Unique Needs

English Language Learners (ELLs) are often grouped together as if they all face the same challenges. But the truth is, they make up one of the most diverse student populations in our schools. When we overlook their differences, it becomes much harder to provide the right support. This article explores the wide range of ELLs in schools today. Of course, it doesn't capture every type of student, but it's a start—and it's important to remember that every student, regardless of how common or uncommon their background may be, deserves the same attention when placed into an ELL program.

People often assume that most ELLs speak Spanish, and while it's true that around three-quarters do, the rest speak dozens of other languages. In California alone, students speak 67 different languages, with Vietnamese, Mandarin, Arabic, and Filipino among the top ones after Spanish. In some cases, teachers work with students who speak Indigenous languages like Mixtec— languages that the teachers may never have encountered before.

But knowing a student's home country doesn't always tell you what language they speak. Even students from the same country might speak different dialects or completely different languages. For example, two students from Mexico might not both speak Spanish, or they might speak different forms of it. That's why classifying students based on country of origin doesn't work.

A better approach is to look at their age, experience, and skill level. One group, for instance, is made up of very young children—dual language learners—who are between birth and age five. Then there are English Learners (ELs), defined by federal guidelines as students who speak a language other than English at home and need extra help becoming proficient.

Within this broader category, there are several subgroups. Newcomer ELs have usually been in the country for less than a year and are just beginning to attend U.S. schools. Long-term English learners (LTELs) have been here for more than six years but still haven't reached full proficiency. Reclassified Fluent English Proficient (RFEP) students have met the English proficiency requirements, passed classroom evaluations, and had their progress reviewed with a parent. Even though they're no longer considered ELs, schools still monitor them to make sure they stay on track. Another group, Initially Fluent English Proficient (IFEP) students, test as proficient right away and are placed in general education classrooms.

Different students need different types of support. One major distinction is between ELLs who were born in the U.S. and those who immigrated later. About 72% of ELLs are born in the United States. Many of them speak English fairly well in daily life, but still struggle in academic settings. They may not have received strong language support in their early education, so they need focused help with academic English. A lot of these students have at least one immigrant parent, and about 750,000 ELLs have undocumented parents. That can cause additional stress, which affects learning. For these students, supportive school environments matter just as much as good lesson plans.

ELLs who recently arrived from other countries have their own set of challenges. Some are what educators call SIFEs—students with interrupted formal education. These students might have missed school due to war, poverty, or other difficult circumstances. They need what's called "survival English," meaning basic language skills that help them get through the school day and function in their communities. They also need time to build up foundational skills in reading and content subjects.

This comparison between native-born and foreign-born ELLs shows how different their needs can be. Even within those groups, no two students are alike. For example, two students might both be LTELs, but one could learn best by listening to lectures while the other does better with hands-on projects. That's why placement shouldn't be based only on a standardized English test. It should include questions about students' backgrounds, their school history, and how they learn best.

There are still more types of ELLs—migratory students who move often due to their family's work, or heritage language learners who understand a home language but don't speak it fluently. The list could keep going. But what's clear is that no single teaching method works for every ELL. It's time to start thinking beyond labels. Classifying students with care and teaching them with flexibility is how we make sure every learner gets what they need.

Allison Zhang

Addressing Deficient Funding and Accountability for ELL Education

The Civil Rights Act of 1964 and the Equal Educational Opportunities Act of 1974 require public schools to provide academic support for English Language Learners (ELLs). These laws make it clear that the federal government has a responsibility to fund such programs. Yet even with these legal mandates, there is still not enough research or clarity on how these funds should actually be distributed. One of the biggest problems is that federal decision-makers often overlook how quickly and dramatically the ELL population is growing—and how much more diverse it has become.

At the heart of the issue is the overall lack of funding for ELL education. When we look at how federal support is broken down, we see five main areas. The first gives grants to schools with high numbers of students from low-income families. The second focuses on the education of migratory children. The third is designed to improve teaching quality through professional development. The fourth supports school districts that serve refugee populations. Only the fifth category specifically focuses on helping ELL students gain English proficiency and succeed academically. That means just one section of the entire federal funding system is truly aimed at the needs of ELLs.

This limited funding puts ELLs at a major disadvantage. According to Diana Quintero, former senior research analyst at the Brown Center on Education Policy, 20 percent of schools enroll nearly 75 percent of all ELLs in the country. The same report shows that 37 percent of ELL students live in poverty, compared to 21 percent of the overall public school population. That means ELLs are often concentrated in high-poverty schools that are already underfunded. Meanwhile, the number of ELL students continues to rise. UnidosUS, a nonprofit organization based in Washington, D.C., reports that the ELL population has

126

grown by 35 percent over the past two decades. At the same time, funding for these students has dropped by 24 percent when adjusted for inflation.

Without adequate funding, schools struggle to provide even the most basic resources for ELL students. A study conducted by the English Learners Success Forum and San Diego State University found that many teachers lacked access to appropriate textbooks and materials for teaching ELLs, especially in math and English. Even when they did have resources, many of those materials were outdated or irrelevant to the students' actual needs.

One reason for this problem is the way funding is studied and evaluated. Most funding models rely on something called "costing out" studies, which use data from standardized tests to estimate how much support students need. However, these studies rarely focus on ELLs. Researchers Oscar Jimenez-Castellanos and Amy Topper reviewed 70 empirical studies and found that only four were centered on English learners. Because of this lack of attention, most funding models don't capture the full scope of what ELLs need in the classroom.

When studies don't accurately reflect the population they're meant to serve, accountability becomes another concern. Right now, most state funding systems do not link funding to measurable goals for ELL progress. Although some lawmakers have called for this kind of accountability, many of their proposals don't explain how the money should be used. In most cases, states provide funds based only on the number of ELLs enrolled in a school. They do not include support for former ELLs—students who still need help even after being reclassified as fluent. As a result, schools may feel pressured to move students out of ELL programs before they're truly ready, just to maintain funding levels.

That said, federal and state governments have taken steps to support ELLs in recent years. For example, when the COVID-19 pandemic hit, Congress allocated nearly $190 million in emergency relief funds for vulnerable students, including ELLs. This funding, part of the Elementary and Secondary School Emergency Relief (ESSER) fund, represented one of the largest federal investments in K–12 education to date.

Still, one-time relief is not enough. Lasting change will require more targeted research and thoughtful policies. One solution is to increase the use of cost-benefit analyses that are tailored to ELLs specifically. These studies need to account for the wide range of experiences, backgrounds, and challenges that ELLs bring to the classroom. No single model will work for every student. In addition, states should set clear annual goals for ELL education, tying funding to progress in a meaningful and transparent way. This will encourage districts to stay focused on student outcomes, not just enrollment numbers.

Finally, even after students are reclassified, they often need continued support. States should consider offering reduced but ongoing funding for these learners, especially those living in poverty. This approach would allow former ELLs to stay on track and feel supported, rather than falling behind once they leave the program.

Meeting the needs of ELL students requires more than temporary funding or broad policies. It demands ongoing research, specific strategies, and a commitment to treating these students as more than just numbers. With better systems in place, we can ensure that all ELLs—no matter their background—receive the education they deserve.

CALP Deficiency Solved by CALLA: Overcoming the Gap Between Conversational and Academic Language for ELLs

In English language learning, there's a key difference between everyday conversation and classroom language. Basic Interpersonal Communication Skills, or BICS, refer to the kind of English people use in casual settings—ordering food, chatting with friends, or asking for directions. Most English learners develop this type of language naturally just by being around it. They pick it up from TV shows, music, or simply talking to people.

But academic English is a different story. Known as Cognitive Academic Language Proficiency, or CALP, it includes the structured vocabulary and grammar found in textbooks, essays, and lectures. This type of language is harder to pick up. It's not something you just absorb through conversation—it takes years of schooling to build. Native English speakers start learning it early, but English learners often arrive without that background, which puts them at a disadvantage.

That's where things get tricky. Some ELLs sound fluent in daily conversation, so teachers might assume they're ready for any classroom. But fluency doesn't always mean full understanding. A student might know how to chat about their weekend but struggle to write a five-paragraph essay or interpret a science passage. When students are placed in mainstream classes without the academic language support they need, they fall behind—sometimes quickly.

The consequences can be serious. In elementary school, the language gap is often masked by simpler vocabulary. But by middle school and high school, the academic language load increases. One researcher involved with the No Child Left Behind Act noticed that many ELLs kept up through early grades, but by fifth grade, their test scores began to drop. According to the Office of English Language Acquisition, the graduation rate for ELLs is about 68%, well below the national average of 87%.

Conversational fluency isn't enough. ELLs need targeted support to build CALP. One effective method is the Cognitive Academic Language Learning Approach, or CALLA. This teaching model was created to help English learners develop academic language while mastering grade-level content. Instead of dropping students into lessons they're not prepared for, CALLA breaks down the material into manageable steps.

The approach emphasizes strategy. Teachers don't just present content—they show students how to learn. For example, instead of handing out a passage and asking students to summarize it, a teacher might model how to identify the main idea, take notes, and ask questions. Students watch, then try the strategy themselves. Over time, they learn how to approach new topics with more confidence.

CALLA follows five steps: preparation, presentation, practice, evaluation, and expansion. In the preparation phase, teachers talk with students about what they already know and introduce key vocabulary. During a presentation, new concepts are introduced, often with visuals or demonstrations. Then comes practice, where students use the strategies they've learned—sometimes working with classmates to apply new skills. Evaluation encourages students to reflect on what they understood and what they struggled with. Finally, the expansion phase connects the lesson to students' lives, helping them see how the content fits into a larger context.

The model has shown real results. In one study by lecturer Desi Tri Cahyaningati, students taught with CALLA scored higher in speaking assessments than those in a traditional classroom. Both groups started at the same level, but the CALLA students made greater gains. Another study by Tina Yaser, an English instructor at Birzeit University, found that CALLA helped students improve their reading comprehension and feel more prepared for standardized tests like the TOEFL.

Developing academic language skills is a long process, especially for students who have had limited exposure to English in school settings. CALLA provides a structured framework that builds academic proficiency gradually and gives students access to learning strategies that can improve their outcomes across subjects. For schools looking to close the achievement gap between ELLs and their peers, it offers a practical, research-backed approach.

Allison Zhang

The Lack of Bilingual ELL Teachers

There are three main instructional models for English Language Learners (ELLs) in the United States. English as a Second Language (ESL) programs focus on full immersion into English without significant regard for a student's native language. Transitional bilingual programs support English acquisition while maintaining instruction in the student's native language. These often include core subjects like math and science taught in a language such as Spanish, the most common native language among ELLs. Dual-language programs divide the school day between English and another language, integrating both native English speakers and ELLs so that each group can acquire a second language.

While ESL programs prioritize faster language transition, research consistently shows that bilingual education—transitional and dual-language models—results in stronger long-term outcomes for ELLs. Though these programs can take longer to yield measurable proficiency gains, often spanning six years rather than the three to five years of ESL, they are more effective overall. Studies from institutions such as George Mason University and the Harvard Graduate School of Education have linked bilingualism to increased academic achievement, improved executive function, and more flexible problem-solving. Students in bilingual programs tend to outperform their monolingual peers in areas like reading, vocabulary, and math.

Despite this evidence, bilingual education is limited by a chronic shortage of qualified bilingual teachers. California serves as a clear example of the mismatch between student demographics and available educators. The California Budget and Policy Center found that while over 1.8 million students in the state speak Spanish at home, only about 7,500 teachers are credentialed to teach in Spanish. For other major languages, the disparity is even wider. Around 68,000 students speak Vietnamese, yet only 30 teachers are certified to instruct in it. Mandarin is spoken by more than 67,000 students, but there are just over 400 credentialed teachers.

The root of this gap is partly systemic. The licensing process for preschool teachers to move into early elementary grades is inefficient and unnecessarily restrictive. Many early childhood educators, who tend to be more linguistically diverse than K-12 teachers, hold relevant credentials, including child development permits and bachelor's degrees, yet face structural hurdles when trying to transition into K–3 teaching roles. To meet requirements, they are often forced to work in unrelated preschool settings that do little to prepare them for supporting ELLs in academic contexts.

More broadly, the bilingual teaching pipeline remains underdeveloped. Even at the preschool level, there are not enough bilingual head teachers. Many bilingual individuals are working in daycare roles or assistant teaching positions instead of leading classrooms. The training infrastructure to help these workers become certified teachers is limited. According to a study from the University of California at Davis, 43% of teachers with a majority-ELL student population had not received any relevant professional development in the previous five years. While California technically mandates that all new teachers be trained to support ELLs, only half of them report actually receiving such instruction.

Addressing this issue requires multiple policy adjustments. California can begin by easing the rigid hour-based requirements for early educators to obtain K–3 credentials. At the same time, it must improve and sustain ELL training so that all educators—not just new hires—receive periodic, evidence-based instruction on teaching multilingual students. Ongoing professional development should be built into the system, not offered as a one-time certification hurdle.

With ELL enrollment increasing and California accounting for 29% of all ELL students nationally, closing the bilingual teacher gap is not just a matter of equity—it is an essential step in maintaining instructional quality across the state.

witness and work

---

*"Language becomes the arbiter between me and others...
Emotion. Learning takes place there, for nothing is real
unless it touches me and I embrace it."*

John Rassias

The Right to Speak

A PROFILE of Marini de Livera, founder of Sisters at Law in Colombo, Sri Lanka

On a humid Thursday in Colombo, just after a monsoon had broken and before the streets fully dried, Marini de Livera stepped into a borrowed office near Maradana Station. The electricity had gone out, so the room was lit by two high windows and a cluster of solar lamps lined up along the sill. She brought a stack of manila folders, a thermos of black tea, and her phone, which she set to silent.

She had come to teach.

The women filed in slowly—some wearing saris, others in faded jeans and t-shirts. A few brought children. Most of them came from job training centers, housing settlements, or church groups nearby. All had signed up for Marini's session: English for Employment.

"Let's begin with sentences," she said, flipping to the first page in a thin, photocopied booklet. "My name is. I live in. I can." She wrote the words on a whiteboard propped against a filing cabinet. No one interrupted. One woman raised her hand. "What is the difference," she asked, "between 'can work' and 'could work'?"

Marini smiled. "That is a very good question."

In her thirty-year career as a human rights lawyer, theater director, and former chair of Sri Lanka's National Child Protection Authority, de Livera has never considered language optional. "English is the access point," she told me. "In Sri Lanka, fluency in English often determines whether you are interviewed or not. Especially for women."

It's not just a matter of diction. In state offices, police reports, hospital forms, and job applications, English appears as both a tool and a gatekeeper. Fluency suggests education, polish, a certain kind of readiness. The women Marini teaches often speak Tamil or Sinhala at home. Some never finished school. Others had worked abroad—in Dubai, Qatar, Malaysia—where English was the expected middle ground. Now, back in Sri Lanka, they were looking for work that paid above minimum wage. Work that required knowing English.

We sat in on the session. "If they ask, 'Do you have experience?'" she said, writing out the question. "You say, 'Yes, I have experience as a caregiver.' Or a cleaner. Or a receptionist. Practice saying it in one breath." They did. She corrected pronunciation only when needed. Otherwise, she focused on structure. "You do not need perfect grammar," she said, "but you do need to be understood."

Later, we took a tuk-tuk to a smaller community site in Kotahena, where Marini had been asked to conduct a drop-in legal clinic. The two programs—legal aid and English instruction—often ran side by side. "When someone comes in reporting wage theft or workplace harassment," she said, "they usually also need help filling out forms. Translating. Preparing to speak with an official."

It was here that she first began integrating English learning into her legal work. "You cannot defend your rights," she said, "if you can't name them in the language the court recognizes."

Her training in law and drama intersect in subtle but persistent ways. In workshops, she uses scripts to rehearse conversations—interviews, inquiries, negotiations. Not to perform, but to practice. "It's not about role-play," she said. "It's about repetition. Hearing yourself say something once, and then again."

In the stairwell outside the center, two young women were reviewing verbs. "Want. Need. Apply. Send." De Livera stopped to listen. "When you say 'I want this job,' you must mean it," she said. "And you must say it so they don't dismiss you."

Marini's understanding of this dynamic isn't hypothetical. Her own career required negotiating the expectations of a legal system built on colonial precedent and bureaucratic delay. She has presented reports to the United Nations and testified at the Human Rights Council. She knows what it means to be heard—and what it costs to be ignored.

Still, her focus has narrowed. "Now I work almost entirely with women who didn't finish school," she said. "That's where the law has the least reach. That's where English instruction matters most."

In 2020, after leaving the NCPA, she founded *Sisters at Law*, a volunteer-run organization offering legal aid and basic English courses. The first sessions were held in her home. Since then, the program has moved into churches, community halls, and, more recently, a mobile classroom—an old van refitted with folding chairs, whiteboards, and an amplifier. "The sound system was a donation," she said. "The girls say it makes them feel like it's something real."

At a community center in Gampaha District, she introduced a young woman named Lihini. "She worked in Kuwait," Marini explained. "Then she returned. She couldn't get hired as a receptionist because her English was too limited. So she came here. Now she's applying to hotel jobs." Lihini nodded but said nothing.

"She will speak when she's ready," Marini said. "The goal isn't confidence. It's competence."

Her manner is straightforward. She corrects errors gently, but without lowering expectations. "No one here is stupid," she said. "They just haven't had consistent access."

This idea of access, not achievement, drives her approach. "There are plenty of women who could do office work, manage files, supervise, even run their own businesses," she said. "But if they don't speak English, they're tracked out. And if they're women, no one reconsiders."

During our final day, I joined her for a review session at a school annex near Battaramulla. At the front of the class, Marini stood beneath a handmade sign that read "ENGLISH FOR LIFE." The students, mostly domestic workers on leave, were reviewing past-tense verbs. She moved between them, checking pages. "We don't prepare them for poetry," she said. "We prepare them for paperwork."

At one point, a woman named Renuka raised her hand. She was quiet, middle-aged, and wore a yellow scarf. "If they ask, 'What is your strength?' what should I say?"

Marini looked up from her notes. "You say, 'I am reliable. I learn quickly. I speak English.'" She paused. "Then you stop. Let them ask the next question."

We walked out after sunset. A light wind had started. The city buzzed with low traffic and television static from open windows. I asked her whether she ever wished she had stayed in formal government. She shook her head. "I work faster now," she said. "And the women remember what we practiced."

She waved down a tuk-tuk. "The hardest thing is knowing your words matter." She climbed in, adjusted the bag at her feet, and gave the driver an address.

And then she was gone, on to the next training, the next room, the next group of women, writing sentences that might finally be read.

"They Know They're Facing Challenges, Yet They're Still Fighting"

A Conversation with Dr. Lu, a professor who has worked on ESL for years, on Teaching English Language Learners

Q: What has been your work or experience with English language learners?

Dr. Lu:

I've taught EL and ELD and foreign language for several years, and I've found that ELs are the same as language learners from any country, and in any language. It's difficult, but rewarding, because in the end, scholars emerge multilingual and better able to cope with the challenges of the adult world. ELD kids are tough; they know they're facing challenges, yet they're still trying, still fighting. And that's why there's no other subject I'd rather teach. Scholars go in and take the ELPAC every year, knowing that they might not pass, yet also knowing that they're giving it their all, and even if they don't reclassify, they *will* show gains.

Q: Why is it important for students to learn English?

Dr. Lu:

In North America and other countries where English is a very common language, its acquisition is immensely useful to young people both in school and later in a professional setting. Further, English is intrinsically an extremely difficult language to learn, so for students to master it, it is necessary to approach learning the language with rigor and fidelity during the K–12 years. The difficulty also means that when scholars do master English, they've sharpened other intellectual tools such as problem solving and rapid, extemporaneous communication capability, which helps them in other school subjects.

Q: Are there any benefits for students who start learning English early on?

Dr. Lu:

Naturally, the younger a student is when they begin learning English, the better it is in terms of mastering the language quickly. It is common knowledge that children are able to pick up and adapt to multiple languages at a young age and code-switch. For example, perhaps one language is spoken at home, but another at school, and a young scholar is able to adapt well to both. This doesn't mean that older children cannot also learn English and master it. I was at a high school level myself before I learned any English at all, and I was able to learn the language. However, by and large, the earlier a scholar starts, the better.

Q: What are some of the most important aspects of learning a new language?

Dr. Lu:

Patience, and the knowledge that you won't be perfect—and that's okay—are really important to keep in mind when learning English, or any language. Especially if one is not a native speaker, it's crucial to accept that your level of skill might not be equal to that of other scholars who've been speaking the native language their whole lives. Just the acknowledgement that you're trying, and giving yourself that space and grace, is hugely important when it comes to learning. In addition, it takes time and real effort. Certainly, if one spends long enough among people who speak a certain language, invariably one gradually picks up at least some—or a lot—of the language. But when we approach learning a language with a plan and clear benchmarks in a school setting, a learner can more accurately see their own progress and appreciate just how far they've come.

Q: What are some of the greatest challenges (personal or societal) for English language learners?

Dr. Lu:

Self-esteem is a big one. It's easy to feel down on yourself if you're struggling with English. As a teenager, I've felt it, too, so I really empathize with our high schoolers who are feeling something similar to what I did at that age. Furthermore, in some places, scholars might feel that others are judging them as somehow being less intelligent than fluent English speakers, simply because they (the EL scholars) haven't reached the same level of fluency yet. So, not only are scholars often facing self-esteem issues because they feel that they are behind their English-only peers, but also that society as a whole might be viewing them as less capable than non-EL scholars.

Q: How can native speakers, specifically high school students, help English language learners?

Dr. Lu:

Native speakers can simply accept English learners as equals; one doesn't have to try to be best friends with ELs in a way that isn't organic, but at the same time, ELs deserve respect, not stigma. Especially with the social, peer pressure of high school, ELs might feel even greater pressure because, in addition to all the normal challenges that teens face when interacting with their peers, ELs have the struggle with English on their shoulders, too. So, native speakers can simply treat ELs like anyone else. ELs don't want special treatment or different treatment; they simply want the *same* treatment. ELD scholars shouldn't be teased for having ELD, any more than any scholar should be teased for taking any class that aids them in their learning journey.

"You Have to Tell Your Own Story"

A Conversation with Asian American filmmaker Tony Shyu on Media, Asian American Identity, and English Language Learners

Q: Can you tell me about your work with Asian American rights?

Tony Shyu: A lot of my work has focused on how media shapes the way people understand Asian American identity. The film industry, especially, plays a powerful role in how stories are told and received. For a long time, the perspective of Asian Americans was distorted, either sidelined or told through the lens of the majority. That perspective often carries certain stereotypes. It's not necessarily malicious, but if someone makes a film about a culture they're not deeply familiar with, some things inevitably become caricatures. That's why it's so important that we tell our own stories through our own lens. Media is one of the most effective ways to reach the public, and we need to use it to represent our communities authentically.

Q: Can you tell me about your experience with English language learners?

Tony Shyu: I've worked with a number of English language learners over the years, and I've seen firsthand how language can sculpt someone's experience in the U.S.—not just in school, but in life. There's this assumption that if you speak with an accent, you don't really understand American culture. And that can be damaging. It creates a bias, especially in professional settings like job interviews or the media industry. Even if someone's lived here for decades, if their English doesn't sound like "American English," people think they're an outsider. That's the unfortunate reality.

Q: How do you think Asian American rights intersect with the experience of English language learners?

Tony Shyu: That's a big question. First, it's important to remember that not all Asian Americans are English learners—many are born here and speak English as their first language. But there's still this underlying stereotype that Asians aren't fluent or aren't culturally "American." That's where the two experiences overlap. If you have an accent or if your English isn't perfect, people assume you're not one of them. That perception affects how you're treated socially, professionally, and politically. In the media world, especially, language and culture are tied together. If you want to be seen as part of the media world, people expect you to perform Americanness. That creates a lot of pressure.

Q: How do you think being an English language learner affects life beyond school?

Tony Shyu: It doesn't end when you graduate. In many ways, that's when it gets harder. In school, you might have support systems—bilingual teachers, ESL classes—but in the real world? You're often on your own. Job opportunities shrink, especially in fields like media or politics, where communication is central. If you don't "sound American," you're often overlooked, even if you're more than qualified. It's about perception, and that perception can be a huge barrier.

Q: What can we do to help English language learners?

Tony Shyu: For one, we need to create more media that reflects their experiences. We're seeing more Asian Americans entering the film industry now, which is a good start. When we tell stories about language, identity, and the challenges of assimilation, it helps non-Asian audiences shift their perception. That kind of cultural dialogue is key. And at the community level, we need to support programs, films, and advocacy work that center these voices.

Q: Are there any organizations you think people should know

about if they care about English language learners or Asian American rights?

Tony Shyu: A few that come to mind are the Asian American Justice League and TAFT—the Asian American Foundation. But I'll be honest: there isn't enough funding going around. A lot of these organizations are competing for the same limited resources, and the Asian American community hasn't always been united. You'll have Filipino Americans, Korean Americans, Chinese Americans... but not always working together. That started to change during the COVID-19 pandemic, when anti-Asian hate brought people together. But we still have a long way to go.

My advice? Start your own thing. Create a club at your school that talks about Asian American identity. Advocate for the issues you care about. Join existing clubs, connect with others. We need more people telling our stories, truthfully, and from within the community.

Allison Zhang

The Bridge Between Worlds
An Interview with Professor Yafen Lo of Cal State University

At a corner table in the education building at Cal State LA, Professor Yafen Lo sits with her hands folded neatly on her lap, the sunlight from the tall windows catching on her wristwatch. "It always comes back to language," she says quietly. "Language is how we begin to see ourselves."

Professor Lo, a longtime educator and advocate for English language learners, is known among her students not just for her scholarship but for her insistence that early childhood education is a matter of both pedagogy and care. "The younger the learner," she says, "the more important the emotional scaffolding becomes."

She tells me that her experience with early childhood development began in the field, not the classroom. "I started by observing," she says. "Watching how language acquisition was happening not only through direct instruction, but through imitation, gesture, rhythm, and relationships." Her work now centers on how bilingualism intersects with identity, how children who are still forming their sense of self also begin forming their linguistic boundaries.

When I ask her about the connection between early development and English language learning, she nods slowly. "The two are inseparable," she says. "Language is not just a tool we use. It's the architecture of thought. So if a child is delayed or limited in one language, it doesn't mean they are deficient. It often means we haven't yet built them the right bridge."

This metaphor of bridges reappears often in our conversation. Especially when we turn to rural Taiwan, where Professor Lo spent several summers working with students who had few formal resources and even fewer teachers trained in multilingual instruction. "They were bright, curious," she recalls. "But without access

146

to books, to fluent models, to encouragement, they internalized the idea that English—and by extension, the outside world—was not for them."

That idea disturbed her. So she built her own bridge.

Her nonprofit organization, which partners with rural schools in Taiwan, began as a modest book donation effort and has since grown into a hybrid learning and mentoring initiative. "I wanted to offer not just textbooks, but relationships," she says. "Not just pronunciation drills, but stories, connection, possibility."

When I ask what we can do—what educators, parents, even peers can do—to better support young English language learners, she doesn't hesitate. "Listen to them," she says. "Slow down for them. Treat their home language as an asset, not an obstacle. Celebrate code-switching as a form of brilliance."

Before our conversation ends, she mentions something that has stayed with me. "The mistake," she says, "is thinking that English should replace. The goal is not to erase the child's first language, but to expand their world."

epilogue

"For last year's words belong to last year's language, and next year's words await another voice. And to make an end is to make a beginning."

T. S. Eliot

Epilogue

Dear Little Me,
Hi, it's me. I mean, it's you. Just a little older. Okay, a lot older.

I want to tell you something really important: you're going to be okay. I promise.

I know school is hard right now, sometimes you don't talk even when you want to, your heart races when the teacher calls on you, and you pretend to drop your pencil just to buy time. I know you think your English is bad. But guess what? It's not.

You're learning a whole new way to speak. That's not easy or small. That's brave.

I remember how you sit at your desk, practicing the same sentence in your head over and over, hoping it comes out just right. Sometimes it doesn't. That's okay. It doesn't have to be perfect. Nobody's is. Even the kids who laugh when you say something a little wrong. They mess up too. They just don't notice it the way you do.

You're afraid that people won't like you if you mess up a word. But people who matter will wait for you to finish your sentence. They'll see how hard you're trying. One day, someone will say, I like how you talk. And they'll mean it.

I know you miss how easy it was to speak in Chinese, how words just came out like water. Here, it feels like walking on rocks. But that doesn't mean you're behind. It just means you're learning how to carry two languages at once. That's something special. That's something strong.

Epilogue

It's okay to be quiet sometimes. It's okay to feel lost. It's okay to cry. Just don't give up.

You will write beautiful things one day. You'll tell stories that make people stop and listen. You'll help others who feel the same way you do right now—shy, small, unsure. You'll help them feel brave.

So next time your voice shakes in class, or you don't know how to say a big word, just take a breath. Look around. You are doing something amazing.

I'm proud of you already.

Love,

Future You
(the one who speaks both languages, and still remembers how hard it was)

Epilogue

"Language is the road map of a culture. It tells you where its people come from and where they are going."

Rita Mae Brown

There are now more than 5 million English language learners in the United States, and that number is growing.

Every day, new students enter classrooms where the curriculum does not speak their language. Where their quietude is mistaken for disinterest, their names are mispronounced, their intelligence underestimated, and their potential deferred.

But every day, too, a child says their first full sentence in English. A parent learns to write a resume. A teenager reads their first novel without translating in their head. Progress is not always linear, but it is always sacred.

This book began as my attempt to remember what I was never meant to forget. The early struggle. The hours with a dictionary. The loneliness of not yet having words for what I felt. But now, it must also serve as a call.

To policymakers: Equity in education must include language access.

To schools: ELL is not a "special case"—it is a central reality.

To teachers: ELL students don't need pity. They need high expectations, scaffolding, and belief.

To peers: Language learners are not behind. They are bilingual. They are bicultural. They are navigating multiple worlds with courage you may never see.

"If you talk to a man in a language he understands, that goes to his head.

If you talk to him in his language, that goes to his heart."

Epilogue

—Nelson Mandela

It is no longer enough to treat English learners as afterthoughts in the classroom or footnotes in education policy. They are the present and future of our schools. They are students, thinkers, creators, and leaders. They deserve to be seen not only for who they are, but for who they are becoming.

This book ends here, but the work continues.

The work of listening.

The work of changing.

The work of translating understanding into action.

Because to support English language learners is not simply to teach a skill.

It is to affirm a life.

—Allison Zhang

www.ingramcontent.com/pod-product-compliance
Lightning Source LLC
Chambersburg PA
CBHW071344090426
42738CB00012B/3008